职场完美措辞系列

成功应对职场困境全攻略

[美]苏珊 F·本杰明◎著　王春生　高　勤◎译

人　民　邮　电　出　版　社
北　京

图书在版编目（CIP）数据

成功应对职场困境全攻略 / （美）本杰明著 ; 王春生，高勤译. -- 北京 : 人民邮电出版社，2013.2
（职场完美措辞系列）
ISBN 978-7-115-30579-4

Ⅰ. ①成… Ⅱ. ①本… ②王… ③高… Ⅲ. ①语言艺术 Ⅳ. ①H019

中国版本图书馆CIP数据核字(2012)第319816号

版 权 声 明

职场完美措辞系列

成功应对职场困境全攻略

◆ 著　[美]苏珊 F · 本杰明
译　王春生　高　勤
责任编辑　李士振
◆ 人民邮电出版社出版发行　北京市崇文区夕照寺街 14 号
邮编　100061　电子邮件　315@ptpress.com.cn
网址　http://www.ptpress.com.cn
大厂聚鑫印刷有限责任公司印刷
◆ 开本：880×1230　1/32
印张：8.5　2013 年 2 月第 1 版
字数：248 千字　2013 年 2 月河北第 1 次印刷
著作权合同登记号　图字：01-2012-8875 号

ISBN 978-7-115-30579-4

定价：32.80 元

读者服务热线：(010)67172489　印装质量热线：(010)67129223
反盗版热线：(010)67171154

·目录·

致 谢

谨以此书献给爱瑞卡！无论你在哪里，无论你做什么，感谢你的包容！

Acknowledgments

To Erika, wherever you are, whatever you're doing, thanks for putting up with me!

第一章
职场困境简析

化解职场困境的七个决定性因素

你如何应对困境？当遇到个性冲突，当财务或名誉陷入危机，当遭遇尴尬甚至更糟的情况时，你该如何处理？当遇到这些事情时，众多的因素决定了你能否应对自如。你当然并不想让事态恶化，希望能扭转局势，但做出的努力最终却是多此一举。你想把事情处理好，但结果却适得其反。如果事情总是如此，那么你着手应对困境前，请先考虑以下七个决定性因素，它们将有助于你获得准确信息，做出正确判断，从而取得最佳结果。

1. 困境可能造成的损失程度

有时，局面可能有些麻烦，但仅此而已。你如果致歉或者做了不必要的妥协，这种过度反应可能会对你不利。反之，不合时宜的冷漠态度也会让人觉得你不友善甚至更糟。因此，一定要先评估局势再做出反应。

2. 涉及到的个性因素

困境所涉及的人与困境本身一样重要，这决定着应对方法。在正式场合遇见古板的副总裁或老学究，你千万不可儿戏；而如果你是面对一群推销员，并且经常与之在酒吧共度周末，那么一句笑话、拍拍后背或一封措辞幽默的电子邮件就是化解困境的灵药。

3. 机构的文化氛围

任何机构都有自己的内部礼节、文化和规则，这些能够界定是非。所以应对困境的方式取决于当时的具体情况。有些地方权力等级森严，有很明确的报告线。想越级找高管讨论与其下属之间的严重问题？想都别想！就算你昨天刚与这些高管共进过午餐也不行。你应该去找直接主管。其他文化因素还包括说话的口气、传递信息的方式、副本抄送的对象以及机构的容忍度，即能否容忍造成困境的行为。当然，在自己的领地比别人的地盘情况简单些，但无论哪种情况都要考虑机构的文化。

4. 应对的最佳时机

应对的时机与应对的方式同等重要。遇到过这种尴尬情景吗？你报告了不准确信息，是等着别人慢慢发现该错误，还是任由其误导他人？这两种做法的后果都会极其危险，此时必须立刻采取措施。要是与某位同事意见相左，也许一切都会过去。或许迟早会风平浪静，这样问题就会更容易解决。警惕自己的本能反应，它很可能是错误的。如果你性格急躁的话，会冒然采取行动解决问题，继续前进。如果你性格内向的话，会瞻前顾后。不要让你的个性影响应对方式，那只是自我取悦。

5. 信息沟通渠道

应该当面讨论问题还是发送电子邮件说清楚？要是众人目睹了情况会如何？沟通渠道的选择是判断应对方式是否有效的关键。例如：在危机时刻你采用发送电子邮件的方式，有些人可能会置之不理；或者在某些情况下，有些人可能会过于敏感而做出错误的反应。另外，书面形式致歉、承认或者解释实质上是制造了一份书面证据，很难说结果是否有利于你。采用私下面谈的方式又如何呢？你的听众转眼就会忘记你所说的。当然，电子邮件和面谈也各有优势，你需要谨慎选择采用何种方式，也可将两者结合，这样将会为你带来福音，避免情况愈来愈糟。

6. 适宜的语气

以上讨论的都是他人的期望要求，以及相关文化的许可要求。在充分考虑上述因素的同时，我们也要考虑自身的特点。如果你是个风趣的人，善于开玩笑，那么活跃的气氛会有所帮助。当然你也许想调整一下自己的行为方式。事情一团糟时，态度应该严肃认真。的确如此。但是请注意：你也许无意之中采用了反常的沟通方式，却自以为那是最佳的方式。大错特错！殊不知他人希望你采用自己惯常的方式，这才是最好的方式。唯一例外的是涉及法律事务时，风趣的调侃或者不合时宜的反应可能会让你面临起诉的麻烦。

7. 你的诉求

这是最后一点，也是最重要的决定性因素，那就是你期望对方的看法和感受，当然最重要的是他们采取的行动。有时你只是想重申善意；有时你可能希望对方采取进一步的行动，比如购买产品、停止传播谣言，或者庭外和解纷争。因此要讲究策略，一定要制订出有效策略，再尽快使用本书提供的完美措辞或者其他方法。

Part One

An Introduction to Difficult Situations at Work

Seven Determining Factors When Addressing Difficult Situations at Work

So how do you address a difficult situation? One where numerous personalities collide? Or the stakes are high—whether involving money or a person's reputation? Or someone, maybe lots of someones, may be embarrassed or worse? Or should you address the situation at all? That depends on many factors. You don't want to leap in, hoping to save the day, and then realize . . . it didn't need to be saved in the first place. Nor do you want to make things better . . . only then to realize (oh no!) you made them worse. So before you say a single word or compose that e-mail, consider these seven determining factors. They'll help you get the right message to the right place, for the best possible result.

1. Damage That the Difficult Situation May Have Created

Sometimes, the situation may be difficult but nothing worse than that. If you overreact, whether by apologizing or offering unnecessary compensation, you may be making yourself look bad. On the other hand, an inappropriately blasé response may cost you goodwill and worse. So before you respond, assess the situation; then make your move.

2. Personality of Those Involved

Who is involved in the situation is as relevant to the way you respond as the situation itself. If you're in a formal environment, say with stodgy senior VPs or abundantly serious academics, better not make light of the situation. But if you happen to be with a bunch of sales guys whom you regularly close the weekend with at a pub, then a joke, pat on the back, or humorous e-mail may be the best antidote for the situation.

3. Culture of the Organization

Every organization has its own protocols, culture, and rules about what is and isn't appropriate. So how you respond to the difficult situation will depend on where you are at the time. Some places are extremely hierarchical. There's a definite pecking order. Want to run to the big-guy-in-charge to discuss a drastically difficult situation with his or her employees? Don't even think of it—even if you just had lunch together the day before. Instead, you'll need to go to the person next in charge. Other culture issues: the tone you use, how you relay your message, whom you cc, and, even, whether the behavior that led to the difficult situation was tolerated in that environment. If you're on your own home turf, the situation is easier than if you're on someone else's, of course. But either way, give it thought.

4. Appropriate Timing of Your Response

When you respond can be as important as how you respond. Have an embarrassing situation, like you gave inaccurate information in a report? Waiting for people to slowly discover it or allowing them to act on bad information can be disastrous. So, yes, address that situation immediately. But what if the situation involves a disagreeable interaction with a colleague? Maybe it will blow over. Or maybe the strong feelings will die back in time and become easier for you to address. Oh, and be careful to check your gut response; it may not be the right one. Are you an impatient type of person? You may ache to leap in, resolve the matter, and move forward. Are you an introvert? You may want to mull it over before taking steps. Don't rely on your personal style to dictate your response; you may only be satisfying yourself.

5. Vehicle for Your Message

Should you discuss the problem in a one-on-one? Send an e-mail? What if lots of people witnessed the situation? The vehicle you choose will be pivotal to whether your response is effective. For example, if you send an e-mail during a crisis, some people may not open it. Or given the circumstances, they may be overly sensitive and react the wrong way. Besides, in putting an apology, admission, or explanation in writing, you're essentially creating a paper trail that could support or undermine you, depending. Say something in person? Then your audience may forget what you said the moment you walk out the room. Of course, e-mails or one-on-one conversations also have their bright sides. You need to determine which one, or combination of vehicles, will make you shine and not fall further into the shadows.

6. Tone That's Appropriate for You

Up until now, we've discussed what other people expect and what the culture allows. But also consider your own style. Are you a fun-loving person? Quick with a joke? Then making light of the situation can help. Of course, you may opt to temper your style; when all goes wrong, seriousness may be in order. No problem, but beware. You may inadvertently adopt an unlikely communications style, thinking that is best. Big mistake! People expect you to be you—and that's the best way to be. Exception: When legal issues may come into play. Then a witty retort or poorly timed response may send you to court.

7. Outcome You Want

This is last and most definitely not least: what you want the recipient of your message to think, feel, and, above all, do. In some cases, you just want to restore goodwill. In other cases, you might want to get him or her to take a next step: purchase a product, resist spreading gossip, or settle a problem out of court. So be strategic, and before you race to use these perfect phrases—or any others—drum up a strategy that brings results.

第二章
职场中常见的尴尬局面

面对现实吧！职场中，人人都会遭遇各种尴尬。工作中总会遇到此类个人麻烦：你做报告时，裤子拉链竟然没拉；你给好友发送电子邮件，抱怨约会对象差劲，结果此内容却群发给了所有人；你刚怒气冲冲地谈论那个让你发疯的家伙，可碰巧他就站在门外。这样的例子不胜枚举。

令人遗憾的是，没有一所大学开设相关课程来教授如何应对此类尴尬局面。在这方面，即使父母也没有多少人生经验可供我们参考。该如何应对？请使用本章提供的完美措辞吧！它们涵盖了所有你能想象到的（也是你不想遇到的）情景。当然，化解困境的关键是困境的性质。

● **假装若无其事。**这种应对方式通常适用于危害较小的困境。此时如果采取其他方式（开玩笑、亲自道歉，或者立即发电子邮件），只会让对方印象更深刻。而你迫切希望他们淡忘此事。以帕特为例，他是一家技术公司的资深副总裁。有一次他给员工做报告以鼓舞士气。会议中途，他放了屁，实在令人尴尬，不过事情的确发生了。

对于此类尴尬局面，帕特就完全可以采取若无其事的方式。谁会真正介意呢？这样就化解了困境。

● **立刻化解困境。**如果尴尬局面会有损你的个人信誉，并且让上级对你产生不良印象，那就必须立刻解决。保持冷静，采用专业方式马上行动。帕特的情形无伤大雅，但是如果同事无意中听到你抱怨客户，或者你对某重要项目大放厥词，情况就严重了。最好直接正式地请求与其见面商议解决。

● **真诚致歉。**如果同事碰巧听到了你的背后议论，此时道歉是最令人难堪的。这甚至比问题本身还让人难堪。依我之见，职场沟通应只限于行为本身，而不要牵扯到个人情感。但是如果同事的确听到了你对其非议，严重伤害了对方的感情，那么简单致歉是不够的。你必须态度真诚，内容明确，抓住时机。

● **开句玩笑**。这是化解尴尬局面的最佳方式。但是必须面对合适的听众。如果帕特的员工有幽默感（的确如此），他们最终会当面或背后为此事取笑他。那么帕特该如何应对？他在会议中停了下来，抬头看着天花板，若有所思问道："有人听见什么动静了吗？"全场哄堂大笑，帕特继续高谈阔论。

以下还有更多的完美措辞。它们适用于你或你的朋友，可化解各种职场困境。

错发私人电子邮件

想给保姆发个便条，却不小心点错了收信人地址。这种问题很容易解决，不过要是其他情况就要另当别论，比如你和妻子在电子邮件中谈论了自己近来的胃病，或者更糟糕的是关于目前紧张的婚姻关系问题。此类邮件涉及细节越多，情况就越复杂。此时最佳策略要依据收件人和你的关系而定，还要考虑此事对工作造成的影响。如果邮件会影响职场生涯，必须处理，反之则可以置之不理。

邮件内容涉及重要个人信息

你希望尽快得到对方的答复，要求他尊重你本人及你的隐私权，并且对邮件内容保密。此时应立刻致歉，再请对方酌情处理。

● 对不起，写给我________的邮件错发给了您。您也看到了，情况比较麻烦。如果您能对此保守秘密的话，我将万分感激。

● 我刚发现把私人邮件错误抄送给了您，实在对不起。如果能帮我保守秘密，我将不胜感激。

● 很抱歉我把写给________的邮件错发给了您。非常感谢您告知我此事，请保密。相信您一定能表示理解。

● 汤姆刚刚告诉我，我把写给________的邮件错发给了您。对不起，给您添麻烦了。您知道这只能给________看。

● 非常抱歉，我刚发现给您发错了邮件。本来是写给________的，您的地址在他的正上方，结果点击时出错了。这封信内容令人不快，涉及隐私，您是否可以不打开阅读而直接删除？

邮件内容无关紧要

此时你的语气可以轻松点，以尽可能消除任何敌意，毕竟你给对方发了垃圾邮件。要是对方能接受，可以增加点幽默。

● 对不起，写给孩子保姆的邮件发给了您。让我想想，如果保姆做不好的话，真的请你来帮忙如何？呵呵！

● 天啊！对不起给你发了垃圾邮件。我并不打算发给你那个邮件。

● 哦，不！________说我不小心把邮件抄送给您了，十分抱歉。

● 出了点技术性的错误，全是我的错。实在对不起，写给孩子保姆的邮件错发给了您。

邮件牵连到他人

无论如何，千万不要为自己开脱，也不用解释发错邮件的原因，只要确保收件人对邮件内容保密，明白你打算亲自处理相关问题，请对方不要插手。若邮件内容涉及对业务发表个人观点，这种方式尤为重要。

● ________刚告诉我您收到我的一封有关弗朗西斯的邮件。请不要让他本人或别人知道此事，好吗？我会尽快与当事人私下沟通此事。

● 我刚发现写给爱迪的邮件错发给您了，请别在意邮件内容。我会马上处理相关问题。

● 如果您收到我的邮件，其中主题词是________，请忽略它。我本来是要发给爱迪的，希望得到他的反馈意见再采取行动。

● 我刚发现自己不小心把本该发给别人的邮件发给您了，请别在意，我只是发泄一下情绪。

你的老板或高管无意中收到此邮件

这种情况不只是令你难堪，还会有损你一贯的优秀员工形象，毕竟优秀员工不应该浪费工作时间处理私人信件。所以你必须首先承认错误，然后解释此类情况很少发生，最后致歉。

- 我刚发现自己不小心把发给________的邮件抄送给了您。您知道我极少占用工作时间处理个人信件，但这次情况紧急，我迫不得已。对此我深表歉意。

- 我检查邮件时发现自己不小心把写给________的邮件发给了您。除非万不得已，我工作时绝不发私人邮件。我希望您能表示理解，出现这种问题实在是对不起。

- 我知道自己错发了有关________的邮件给您。我通常只用家里电脑处理私人邮件。要是您想与我讨论此事，请随时通知我。

- 您可能注意到了我的邮件，其主题为“________”，与业务完全无关。我不小心发送给了您。当时事发突然，否则我会等到回家之后发送它。对不起，但请相信我的绝大多数时间都是用在业务上的。

小提示

你知道不该在工作时间发送个人邮件，但是面对现实吧！你绝大部分时间公务缠身，总会有身不由己的时候。但是请记住：尽量让邮件听上去专业点，仅陈述必要的信息，避免谈论容易惹麻烦的或者不确定的想法和感受。

错误用语：就这点来讲，你是我见到的最大的傻瓜！你竟敢如此对我？别打电话、别发邮件。滚开！

正确用语：你的行为令人无法接受，我不想再和你保持联系了！

私人电子邮件被错误地群发

我有个朋友供职于政府敏感部门。她陷入了热恋，对方来自另一个与美国关系极为敏感的国家。两人之间的情感经历了种种波澜起伏，比两国外交沉浮还要汹涌澎湃，但最终还是分道扬镳。男方后来与别人结婚了。起初一切正常，可随后我朋友发现自己难以自拔，她还深爱着那个男人，迷恋着他。于是她不太得体地写了一封情书，其中极尽哀求之词。她万万没有想到在对方国家里任何人都能看到别人的邮件，结果她的私人邮件被对方公司所有人过目。

应对方式取决于所处的职场文化、所发邮件造成的严重后果（或者可能引起的尴尬程度）以及是否会牵连到他人。很可能该邮件会通过抄送人列表流传开来，并且收件人很可能会将其传播。因此，有时需要有人来处理此事。我朋友的案例中，她本人不需要回应，她的前男友处理了此事。他做了如下回复："我只想让你知道：你同我以及我的所有同事分享了你的情感。现在我的婚姻很幸福，我和这里所有人都祝你好运。"

完美措辞：发件人适用

邮件对原收件人不利

首先为意外发送邮件表示歉意，然后请采用如下常用句式：

- 此邮件决不代表________的观点。我也要向他道歉。
- 请注意邮件内容仅代表我个人观点。
- 我本人对这些观点负全责，它们绝非________的观点。
- 我只是一时冲动才表述了这些看法。这绝对不能完全反映我或者________的观点。

邮件对第三方不利

同样先道歉，再采用以下常用句式：

- 这些看法完全是断章取义，决不应给任何人带来不利影响，尤其是________。
- 这些纯属个人观点，并未与其他人达成共识。
- 如果您看过我的电子邮件，请理解这纯属个人观点，仅限于此。
- 显而易见，如果您对此邮件有任何疑问，可以与________一起进行澄清。

邮件对收件人的工作单位不利（糟糕！）

致歉，然后立即说明邮件的来龙去脉。态度要恭敬，特别是邮件会影响收件人的职位或者工作的其他方面时。

- 您知道我对您的工作单位不太熟悉，所以我的观点不合时宜。
- 我对您单位的看法丝毫没有受到________的影响。您应该直接询问她的意见，千万不要依赖我的观点。
- 我绝对无意冒犯您，我的想法都是断章取义，并且仅代表我个人观点。

小提示

这种情况下，你应该邀请收件人与你直接对话（如果对方愿意）。

完美措辞：收件人适用

前文所述是针对发件人的用语。对于收件人，以下用语和策略可以适用：

幽默法

- 哦，很抱歉！你们并不该看到这些邮件！
- 伙计，你看到就行了，千万别说出去！
- 就当我是想与 100 个密友（碰巧都是在我抄送列表上）分享私人邮件，很抱歉！
- （假装对此邮件毫不知情）什么邮件？

直白法

- 很对不起，那封邮件________只想让我一个人看。
- 你知道我的境况并不像________所说那样。很抱歉在网上打扰你。
- 你知道这是私人邮件，很抱歉在工作时间处理私事。

为客户制定的方案中出现了其他客户的名称

职场中，方案策划有两点是众所周知的：其一，没人会从头做起写方案。事实上果真如此的话，那就无法完成任何工作了，或者一个季度只能完成两三个方案而已；其二，每个人都假装自己的方案是全新的、独一无二的，是为最有价值的潜在客户量身订做的。如果你不小心在客户的署名位置上填写了别的客户名称，那你就揭穿了一个行内皆知的秘密。多数情况下，这种错误令人尴尬，而且与其他小问题一样，这将有损于潜在客户对你的友好印象。当然，如果言辞得体的话，这也是你展示自我的大好机会。大可借鉴以下完美措辞：

首先承认存在问题，以此控制客户的反应

- 我们刚刚发现给贵公司的方案中错用了其他公司的名称。
- 抱歉，由于疏忽，在方案中使用了其他公司的名称。
- 我的同事________（与贵公司洽谈本项目的联系人）刚刚通知我们，在专属贵公司名称的地方错填了其他公司的名称。
- 谨此通知您，由于某种原因，在为您制定的方案中错误地写上了________公司的名称。

如果觉得合适的话，可以致歉

- 实在对不起，我对出现此类错误深感惭愧。
- 我很抱歉，不知道怎么会犯此类错误。
- 非常感谢您指出了我的错误，我真是昏头了。
- 我为此错误深感惭愧。感谢您为我指出了这一错误。
- 这真是个天大的错误，非常抱歉。

若此方案确实是为该客户量身订做的

- 我方团队专门为贵公司开发了此方案，但在后期安排了一名实习生做最终校对工作。由于我公司最近起草了一份类似的方案，她可能把两者

混淆了。我们对此深表歉意。

- 您可能知道，我们确实剪切并粘贴了一些核心业务的段落。但是方案的主要内容确实是为贵公司量身定做的。
- 由于某种原因，我们的一些模板内容出现在了贵公司的方案中，非常抱歉。
- 我们套用了同类方案中的一些内容，由于某种原因，该客户的名称也出现在了本文案中。

方案确实独一无二，但客户名字出错

指出该客户方案中的特别之处，尤其是你以同样的价格提供额外服务的方面。要指出相关条款的具体位置。

- 请您注意第 8 页关于费用明细的部分，我们还为所有的服务提供了九折优惠。
- 正如方案中所述，我们将免费提供额外服务（参见第 4 页第 3 段）。
- 由于我们长期合作，将免费为您提供二级规划，详见方案中的细则部分。
- 如果您需要更多时间来完成此项目，我们将灵活处理。您知道通常这种情况下，我们要加收 10% 的费用，但对贵公司我们是免费的。您可以联系我了解更多的细节，也可以查阅方案最后一部分有关折扣的内容。

小提示

多数人看方案都是一扫而过。他们只关注特定内容（多数和费用有关），然后就放在一边了。所以很可能对方还没有读到或者没有注意到这个错误。如果是这样，那就不要指出来，忽略这个错误，并且希望情况一切顺利。如果确定客户发现了错误，那就使用上述完美措辞。

现场演示时发现错误，运用以下完美措辞

应对方式取决于听众类型。如果可能的话，开句玩笑。

- 喔！瞧，你们什么时候改的名？

● 哼！你们真是________公司（错用的公司名称）的吗？我知道有个公司也叫那个名字？

● 怎么回事？

● 对不起，真难为情。让谁感到难堪呀？或者用职业态度严肃处理，就像你写电子邮件时那样。

以下还有两个例句。

● 抱歉发生此类错误。我们为每个客户起草专用方案，但有时会套用个别段落。

● 名称出现错误，实在对不起。

无论如何，一定要指出该客户独享的优惠条件，确保你明确指出了相关段落或行数，这样能保证客户记住相关内容，并且感觉到特殊的优待：

● 在此提醒您一下，请注意第 3 页包含了我们为贵方项目讨论的所有特定条款。

● 占用您一点时间。请看第 6 页，我提供了双方讨论过的所有折扣。请贵方不要认为这个方案完全是个复制品。

老板无意中听到你对职场中人员和事情的批评言辞

哦，伙计！这可不是你想让老板听到的。但是事已至此，你给自己最不想冒犯的人留下了相当坏的印象，所以最好尽快处理此事。以下完美措辞会有所帮助：

引入主题

● 我想您也许碰巧听到了我的微词。我希望澄清一下当时的情况。

● 我昨天发表了些言论，不知能否与您就此进行简单沟通？

● 您可能听到我说的一些愚蠢言论。我们能否谈谈？

● 我有个问题想占用您 5 分钟时间可以吗？我想您昨天已经听到了我与________对此事的讨论。

● 我有些重要的事希望能与您面谈，不知您的日程表是否有空安排此次谈话？

希望对自己的言论进行解释

● 如您所知，我有时需要发泄情绪。昨天我对________所言只是发脾气而已。

● 我最近一直有些沮丧，需要倾诉一下。

● 我需要听取________的建议，以便圆满完成这一项目，所以我才讨论这些问题。有些事情进展得不太顺利。

● 我发表了一些苛刻的批评性言论，但是归根结底，我认为一切都会好起来。

● 我认为这件事没有那么重要，还不至于惊动您，但我的确需要在工作中与人商谈此事。

你正在讨论一个具体项目

● 我以前承担过类似项目，知道一切都会好起来的。不过首先我必须处理一些影响进度的事情。

● 这个项目遇到一系列特殊情况，很有挑战性。不过，毫无疑问，我正集中精力做好它。

● 我清楚要付出努力才能圆满完成此项目，但是目前我迫切需要投入精力处理这些日益严重的错误。

● 我开始做这个项目时，并没有预见到这些不足之处，因此现在正想方设法解决相关问题。

● 这些问题很严重，不过我对本项目仍然保持乐观态度。

你正在议论其他同事

● 我想________和我之间有些个人问题。我难以与他直接沟通，所以只能向别人倾诉。

● 尽管我觉得________和我之间关系紧张，但我们共事还是很有成效的。

● 我知道自己不是他的主管，也不愿意直接告诉他这些问题。这就是我找________讨论的原因。

● 希望您能了解________会偏向于________，所以我去找________解决烦恼。我知道他会态度公正。

● 总的来说，我和________共事很愉快。但是他时常惹我生气。

你在谈论自己的老板（天啊！）

● 我意识到应该直接向您请示问题。

● 我在这儿工作得相当愉快，发牢骚只是想澄清一些问题并获得反馈意见。

● 我并不愿意麻烦您处理这些事情，不过那也许是更好的选择。

● 我认为这些事没什么了不起，我只是迫切需要倾吐心中的烦恼。

● 请不要以为我会经常那样抱怨。这件事情已经成了我的烦心事。

你正在批评某人，后来发现当事人可能听到了

也许你正交谈时却发现当事人就在门外；也许你参加一次电话会议时，自以为挂断了电话，觉得其他人都已离开现场，结果发现有人一直在洗耳恭听。这让人恨不得钻进地缝。但是等一等，那人真的都听到了吗？对方是否没挂电话就离开了？你有勇气当面提这个难堪的话题吗？你敢于回避这个问题吗？以下完美措辞可帮助你化解这类顶级尴尬困境。

当你无法确定当事人是否听到相关内容

你必须要仔细观察。如果你谈论的话题很平常，那就没什么可担心的，你的评论会烟消云散。如果对方不理睬你或者避开你的目光，那么请用以下完美措辞控制局面。行动要快，你当然不想扩散敌意。

● 你有什么事想要和我谈吗？

● 你有什么重要的事需要和我一起讨论吗？

- 你还好吧？（简单的话语是良好的开场白。）
- 你对我们昨天的谈话有什么想法吗？
- 我能为你做点什么？

当你确定对方已经听到，想开诚布公地沟通

- 我非常乐于讨论昨天我们所说的话。
- 我承认我们的评论有些伤人，但是请别当真。
- 如果你想与我讨论我们所说的话，请通知我。我们并无他意。
- 我为我们的言论表示歉意。你知道当时我们只是想发泄一下。
- 我们受够了所有这些压力。拿你发泄，实在对不起。
- 你知道事情总是会失控的，对吧！这只是一次意外，对不起。

如果你的评论是恶意的，并且与工作无关

道歉不是由于不得已，而应该是出自本意。在职场中发表冒犯他人的言论只会自找麻烦。

- 对我们所说的话感到十分抱歉，都是些胡言乱语。
- 我为我们的言论感到难堪，这并非我们的本意。
- 我们决不该那样议论你，我们太蠢了。
- 我为所说的话道歉，我们太过分了。
- 我为我们先前所说的话感到惭愧，请接受我的道歉，那是完全错误的。

你的评论是关于当事人的工作表现

如果确是你的本意

- 抱歉你是以这样的方式听到了我的想法，我们也许该当面谈谈这些事。
- 我也许应该去和老板（而非其他同事）讨论这些事。
- 很抱歉你是以这样的方式听到了我的观点，但我真的认为你需要认真考虑一些问题。

若并非你的本意

- 对不起，我只是在发泄，拿你当了出气筒。
- 这个项目让我发疯了，这确实不关你的事。
- 事后我马上就后悔了。
- 我并不真是那样想的。请权当是一种发泄吧。

小提示

承认自己不该在职场中议论他人于事无补。你当然是会这样做的，人人都会如此。通过这种方式，你不仅能处理好问题，还能得到有益指点，同时又能发泄怒火。但是请牢记以下两点：第一，议论的内容可以有关业务，也会有恶意内容。但不要恶意取笑他人的容貌、举止以及配偶；第二，要谨慎。应该只与这种人交谈——他们不仅能保守秘密，也可以提供有益的和专业的反馈意见。要确保你们是私下交谈，也就是说不能在自助餐厅里，那样可能会被不该听的人听到。也不要在饮水机旁（或诸如此类的地方）。慎重选择时间，找个安静的地方小声说。

听到了同事对你的非议

这种情况比尴尬还要糟，这很伤人。所以应该仔细考虑，发现有人背后议论自己后，你去找对方的目的是什么？是想澄清自己的看法？是想获取有关同事言论更准确的信息？还是想告诉他们别再说三道四了，把精力用在正路上？以下这些完美措辞可以处理所有这些情况。

但是在采用它们之前，自问一下这些问题：这些议论对我的职业生涯有何影响？你不想做出过激反应，也不愿错过此次机会以搜集关于个人的有益信息（尽管有点让人难以接受）。还有，解决这一问题的最佳场所在哪里？如果想用电子邮件的话，切记它们将会被保留下来，如果你言辞过激的话，这些证据会对你不利。最后，你应该找谈话参与者中的哪个人？是最可能成为盟友的人，还是对方的领头人？

一旦你有了明确的对策，就可以使用以下的完美措辞来达成自己的目的。

澄清自己的观点

首先清楚地表明自己的意图，然后请你的同事参与对话，别让自己听上去过于戒备（当你怒火中烧时，做到这一点并不容易）。如果合适的话，具体讨论所听到的细节。

- 我无意中听到你与________的谈话，内容是你们如何看待我在此项目中的贡献。我想解释一下我的处事原则，这样你就能更加清楚我的动机以及我预期的成果。
- 关于我对“……”的贡献方面你有保留意见，对此我表示理解。我愿意与你讨论一下这个问题，这样你就能明白我的目标了。
- 既然我们每天共事，我想应该和你讨论一下我的工作方式，这样你能更好地理解该对我抱有什么样的预期以及原因何在，我知道你有一些保留意见。
- 我觉得有必要和你谈一下目前为止我对“……”所做的贡献，你也许不了解我的动机，我想确保我们的合作能够取得尽量多的成果。

小提示

不要使用激烈的言辞，以免使对方疏远或使关系进一步恶化。记住，你是想化解此事而不是火上浇油。

错误用语：

- 你所说的都是谎言，最好闭嘴。
- 你说了对我十分粗鲁无礼的话。

正确用语：

- 我理解你在“……”方面有保留意见。
- 我希望澄清一切并且结束分歧。

如果是发送电子邮件的话，粗鲁的或者过于情绪化的词语会被视为骚扰，将对你不利。

获得对方言论的确切内容

尽量给对方提供一次机会与你讨论此事，这不一定有用，但一定要记住不能强迫对方。

● 当你和________谈话时，我无意中听见提及了我的名字，你想不想和我讨论些什么？

● 我听见了你和________的谈话，语气好像不大愉快。我想多了解你们的想法，这样有助于消除可能存在的分歧。

● 你和________可能心存芥蒂，我很想知道存在的问题，这样我们就可以解决它。

● 如果你对我有任何意见，请直接对我说，否则于事无补。

● 既然我们每天一起工作，我们就该开诚布公地谈论分歧。我碰巧听到了你和________的谈话，如果你能告诉我你的想法，将会对情况有益。

让同事停止非议

如果你无意中听到同事说了粗鲁的、不合时宜的甚至是诽谤性的言论，最好是发个电子邮件，这样你就能留存一份书面证据。如果你更乐于面谈，也要在随后发个电子邮件记录相关谈话内容。无论如何，要尽量详细地注明日期及谈话者的言论。如果有人提醒过你注意这些言论的话，也要在邮件中注明。以下这些完美措辞都是使对方停止非议的有效手段。

● 我昨天无意中听到了你和________在自助餐厅里议论我，当时你说我是________和________，我没有听完谈话的其他部分，只是想提醒你这些观点都是主观臆断的、恶意的并且不适于工作场合。

● 有多人提醒过我注意你曾在我的“……”和“……”方面诋毁我。这样做在职场中是不合适的，并且有损于我的名誉。如果你对我的业务表现不满意的话，请直接告诉我。如果你对我个人有异议的话，那就请不要到处宣扬。

● 本周你有好几次拿我取笑，尤其是在“……”和“……”方面。这样做不利于工作并且会造成隔阂，你必须马上停止这种行为。

向客户催款，但实际上对方已经付过了

如果你经营着一家小公司并且发生了现金流转问题，这种尴尬情况会经常发生（尽管你可能不愿承认）。当然，即使你供职于一家大公司，现金流转问题也是最为重要的。你一次次地开账单，一次次地等待，并且得到承诺说支票马上就要寄出了。最后你忍无可忍，发送了一封言辞激烈的电子邮件。就得这样做，这个客户活该，对吧？不过，结果却是在你的文件柜里发现了一个皱巴巴的信封，写着该客户的回信地址，并且——装着一张支票！或者情况更糟：你的会计上周就把支票入账了，却忘了告诉你。试试下面这些完美措辞。

若付款刚刚到达

如果支票确实晚到了，谢谢你的客户并继续敦促对方。

● 我在邮件中提及的那笔付款我方刚刚收到，并且已经入账。

● 谢天谢地，我给您发出邮件后不久付款就收到了，我们会很快入账。

● 我在电子邮件中提到付款已经晚了三周，随后不久我方就收到了该账款。

● 我方已收到你方支付的 6 月 5 日的服务费。如你所知，你方仍拖欠 6 月 10 日和 6 月 15 日的账款未付。

若付款在一两周前就到了

这种情况下你可以道歉。客户的确拖延了，但不像你想象的那么晚。另一方面，礼貌的道歉有利于清除遗留问题，可以使今后的资金流转更快一些。

● 我公司的会计刚刚通知我们已于 6 月 1 日收到了支票，感谢贵方的付款。

● 根据我方记录，实际上我方已于两周前就收到了款项，我们曾错误地发送了催款信息，很抱歉。

● 我方曾向您发送电子邮件催促一笔拖延的款项，事后才发现已于 5

月 19 日收到了该款，感谢您的关注。如果我方先前的邮件给您带来任何干扰的话，我们深表歉意。

● 我们已于 6 月 1 日收到了那笔 5 月 19 日到期的款项，贵方的账务现已结清，我们为最近所发的电子邮件表示道歉。

若是账务系统出现故障，而且你根本没有提供过该项服务

需要道歉吗？当然，而且速度要快，态度要谦恭。

● 刚刚发现我方账务系统的一个错误，我正为一项根本不存在的服务向您索要付款，我对此错误给贵方带来的不便深表歉意。

● 请接受我们的道歉，在检查我方账目时发现我们为一项不存在的服务向您索要付款，我们已经在系统中改正了这一错误，并再次表示歉意。

可能的话开个玩笑

● 我们刚刚意识到发票 B-202 所列的业务根本没有发生，这就是贵方付款迟迟未到的原因！请接受我们的道歉。

● 天哪，我们刚刚发现账目上的一个小错误，我们正在向您讨要一笔根本不存在的欠款。所以，很抱歉打扰了。当然，如果你们真想付款的话……

你当众慷慨激昂地强调一个观点，紧接着却发现自己弄错了

此类困境包含多种层次的尴尬局面。最轻微的是你在与同事和朋友们（但愿如此）开会时犯了此类错误，并且立即有人指正了。糟糕一点的是你正作为权威人士在会上发表讲话，有人意见与你相悖，而且你意识到那人才是正确的。最糟的（也是最令人尴尬的）是你在一个座无虚席的大厅里做报告，在答疑时有一位听众指正了你先前提到的一个观点，场内的其他一些听众（大声地）赞同该人。这时该怎么办？如果你掌握了以下完美措辞的话，那你很幸运。

如果有人在小范围内（聊天室、抄送电子邮件或者是面对面会议）指正你的错误

表示谢意，并且询问对方能否提供有所帮助的信息，这将有助于你重新控制局面并且证明你是地道的专业人士。

● 对您的指正深表谢意，您觉得我该如何获取更多相关信息?

● 这的确很有帮助，您是从哪里得到这一信息的?

● 感谢您能指出这一点，这将使情况有所改变。

● 这将有助于我在进入下面的话题时，阐明自己的观点。

● 我还没发现这一点，感谢您能指出。

当你以权威形象出现时有人指正你

衷心地接受指正，这样可以赢回主动权。最重要的是要诚心诚意。然后继续讨论（或者是在聊天室发言、发博客或是电子邮件）。

● 完全正确，感谢您的指正。

● 既然提到了这一点，是的，你完全正确。感谢你的参与，现在我们说下一个问题。

● 好主意，让我们看看这将如何影响后面的论点。

● 感谢您纠正我的观点，下面我们要讨论……

● ________对我的博客发表了评论，他正确地指出了……

● 贵期刊发表的“……”观点，即“……”本该是“……”，是正确的。我很欣赏这一反馈，然而我的结论没有变，理由在于“……”。

在同事之间

如果你们工作关系密切，并且彼此参加过对方的婚礼和国庆节聚会的话，那你完全可以用个人的方式解决，适当的时候可以开个玩笑缓和一下气氛。

● 对不起，伙计们，他是对的。

● 噢，你是对的。我怎么就不知道呢?

● 实际上________这次又对了，让我们继续吧。

● 好主意，的确很棒。（简单一点更好。）

与客户之间

在接受指正的同时强调自己观点的合理性或者其贡献的最终价值。这可以维护你的信誉。

● 我很欣赏________在今天早些时候所发电子邮件中的观点，请注意这一变化并不影响我们的最终结果。

● ________正确地指出了"……"，幸运的是，这意味着你们实际上可以从我方获得更多的"……"。

● 尽管________确实提出了一个重要观点，但多数的专业人士都同意我的原始数据也是可用的。

● 我已经将________所作的修改录入到我们的分析中，而且正在发送修改版。

你在报告中提供的事实或者建议被发现是错误的

太糟了，你写了一份报告，并且将其发送给你的客户、团队或者老板。这是一份关于未来情况的确定性说明，而且结论取决于你的观点。原本一切正常，直到你做出的预测、陈述的事实以及天晓得其他的什么内容被证明是错误的。尴尬吗？毫无疑问。所以首先承认错误，适当时对指正你的人表示感谢。可使用以下完美措辞。

● 很抱歉那份报告中出现了错误。

● 感谢您告知我那份报告中存在的问题，我深感遗憾，真不知这是如何发生的。

● 非常感谢您能在第一时间告知我这份报告中包含的错误信息。

● 和团队中的其他人一样，我对该报告检查了好多次，所以我对发生这样的错误感到惊讶，真是让人难堪。

● 我对报告中的错误信息表示歉意，其实我认真地复核了信息，当我有疑问时总会向他人求证。

然后提供一些补救的方案来弥补自己的错误，确保你的补救措施足以抵消你的错误。如果该错误导致客户损失了金钱或者时间，那就尽量免费提供一些服务。如果报告是提交给老板或者内部人员的，要向他们表明你如何检讨了自己的工作方法以确保不再发生此类错误。无论如何，要尽可能改正错误。以下完美措辞会有所帮助：

对老板

- 我回去再次检查报告，并且会在下周一用电子邮件给您提交新的版本。
- 今天下班后我会把团队召集起来再次检查报告。
- 我会把编制报告的流程再次梳理一遍，以确定出错环节，并确保今后不会再出错。
- 请相信我的确是力求正确并且反复核查了所提供的事实。我会找到出错环节并立即向您汇报。

对客户

- 我们为我方报告中的错误感到惭愧。我们会马上给您发送修订版，并免费向您提供帮助以落实改正措施。
- 您在邮件中要求额外的10个……作为这些错误的补偿，我们很乐于提供15个。
- 我们已经仔细检查了该报告，下周一一大早就给您发送修订版，我们还将免费为您延长一个月的服务。
- 谨向您承诺：此类问题极少发生，实际上就我所知仅此一例。我很乐于同您或贵公司的任何人协商改进措施，并寻求进一步解决此问题的方法。

对同事

- 我会重新检查报告，并且用电子邮件给每个人发送修订版。
- 我很乐于修改其他报告以反映此变化，并且最晚在周五给你发送一个复本。

● 对不起伙计们，告诉我下一步该怎么做来进行补救。

● 你们知道我是很认真核对事实的，如果有谁能指点我如何改进的话，将不胜感激。

当然，有时错误并不严重，只是让人有点尴尬而已，这种情况下道个歉就可以了。

● 非常感谢您指出第 6 页上的错误，我已改正过来了。

● 感谢您的反馈，谢谢。

● 我也不清楚这个错误的数据是怎么出现在这里的，感谢您能指出来。

● 对您所做的改正万分感谢。

小提示

“道歉”是一种微妙的行为，它可能只是告知对方你对这一错误感到遗憾，但也可能会使一个原本平常的错误被极度放大。所以一定要小心防止过度道歉，否则可能会引起对该问题不必要的过分关注。在某些行业还可能更糟——会让你惹上官司！比如，我担任顾问的一家公司里，有个卡车司机在从小路上向外倒车时意外撞到了其他车辆。幸运的是没有导致死亡，但是有两位乘客受伤，并且被撞车辆也彻底报废了。该公司受到当地报纸的批评。他们本该只是做个简短的道歉，并且向公众保证其所有驾驶员都已被责令参加安全驾驶培训，如此即可。然而这家公司却反复不断地为伤者所受的精神和肉体痛苦而致歉，并且（作为一家有人情味的公司）表达他们为此是如何地痛心疾首。这一错误的公开表态使该公司在案件审理中损失惨重。

偶尔（明显地）打嗝、呻吟或者放屁（这的确时有发生）

在职场上应该表现得专业、庄重，并且彻头彻尾地非人格化。必须面对的是：存在着各种各样微妙的规则限制着我们的一切行为。在焦渴难耐时不能将汽水一饮而尽，而是要仔细地、缓慢地呷；不能痛快地打嗝（尽管这种感觉非常棒），而是要闭上嘴唇，不要发出任何不得体的声音；至于着装，男士们即使是在炎热的夏天也必须穿西服、系领带，女士则必须穿职业套装（或者是带有死板袖子的服装）；如果在外衣上有一块汗渍（尤其是在腋下的话）……喔！太令人尴尬了！

得了，理智一些吧！这些事就像呼吸一样正常，没什么可尴尬的。若你仍然难以释怀，那么以下这些简短而有效的完美措辞将帮助你处理此类情况。

刚放了个屁或者感到马上要放屁

如果你是一位男员工，并且和一帮哥们儿一起工作，那么以下这些完美措辞将会尤其“完美”。通常它们不适用于男女成员都有的公司。

- 为了你的安全，请离开现场！我要放屁了！
- 啊！真恶心，我刚才放屁了吗？抱歉，伙计们。
- 哇！真扫兴！
- 快开窗，关上你们的门！

记住，这种方式只适用于那些童心未泯的人，若非如此，请采取更加正式和真诚的方式。

- 抱歉，我这几天肠胃不适。
- 抱歉，真不该这样！
- 对不起，伙计们，我忍不住了！
- 请原谅。

当众打嗝

这只会让对方耳朵不舒服而已，没多大危害，所以简短地致歉即可。

- 对不起，伙计们。
- 原谅我。
- 请原谅。
- 请谅解。
- 呀！真对不起。

意识到没拉拉链（尤其是在当众讲话时）

设想一位大学老师正在兴高采烈地给五百多个学生讲课。你猜怎么着？在 90 分钟的授课过程中他的拉链一直敞开着！该怎么办呢？

可以开个玩笑

- 只是想凉快一下。
- 想吹吹风。
- 请原谅，今天穿衣时正在思考本次讲课内容。以后我会更加注意。

或者正式道歉

- 请原谅，……
- 对不起，你们能否……（一边说一边拉上拉链）

若你事后得知此事

可以在下次双方见面时谈及此事，语气轻松一点，并且重新掌控局面。这里提供一些例句，但在实际中如何使用要取决于你的讲话内容。

- 我们必须注意细节，比如说，别忘了拉拉链。
- 要确保提案看上去完全专业化，像没拉拉链这样的问题只会让我们难堪。
- 当然，我们总是乐于原谅一些无心的行为不慎，比如说没拉拉链。

在主持会议或讲话时发现腋下有汗渍

可以直言不讳

- 看起来炎热的天气损害了我的衣服。
- 请原谅我的衣着，我知道这不是时下流行的。

也可委婉言之——对方能明白你的真实想法

- 实在太热了，你们呢？
- 天啊！这可真热。

也可避而不谈

小提示

如果要在事后重提某一尴尬场景的话，首先要确定对方已经注意到并且记住了此事，否则的话还是不提为妙。

叫错别人的名字

与很多尴尬场景一样，这并没什么大不了的。没人受到伤害，也不存在蓄意冒犯，基本上一切正常。如果不是对方做出反应的话，你根本不会意识到。当你叫错了他们的名字（或者更糟——发错了音）时，他们的反应就像是挨了一记耳光一样。你怎么敢这样！竟敢叫错我的名字！如同你当众侮辱了他们一样！这种情况下你必须好言抚慰。使用贴切的完美措辞，其效果会超出你的想象。

在会议中或者是在引荐时叫错名字

- 对不起，您使我想起了一个同名的人。
- 是的，当然。抱歉我忘了。
- 你使我想起了……
- 我总是记不住名字，但是我对您的相貌以及我们先前的谈话内容记忆犹新。
- 抱歉，那才是我想说的。
- 谢谢，我也不知怎么给弄混了。

在电子邮件中写错名字

- 抱歉，我应该知道的。
- 写错了您的名字，很抱歉。
- 感谢您改正了我的笔误。

- 感谢您的指正，我认识一个人，他与您同名但写法不同。
- 感谢您能告诉我，从现在起我一定会写对。

有人指出你在白皮书、简报或者博客中写错了别人的名字

- 感谢您指出这一问题，如您所见，我已经在博客中改正了。
- 感谢您提醒我注意这个错误。
- 感谢您通知我，我竟然弄错了如此重要的细节。

在下一期内容中指出这一错误及其改正措施：

- 我们在博客中意外地写错了市长的名字，正确写法是“……”。
- 在 2008 年夏季的简报中，我们写错了顾问的名字，应该是“……”。
- 1990 年至 1996 年担任大使的姓名应该是________，我们将在今后的解说词和出版物中改正过来。

读错对方的名字

- 能请您重复一遍正确的发音吗？这样我就能马上改过来。（然后重复一遍正确的发音。）
- 抱歉，您说的是“……”（重复正确的发音）吗？
- 我还不知道呢，谢谢您告诉我。
- （重复正确的发音）这样说对吗？谢谢。

当拿不准对方名字的发音时，请询问

与其事后道歉不如事先询问，而且，询问对方名字的正确发音可以表达你的尊重、礼貌和关心。

- 可否教我如何正确读出您名字？
- 我已经知道您的名字了，该如何正确发音呢？
- 这样读您的名字对吗？……
- 请问您的名字是怎么读的？我想把音发准。

Part Two

Embarrassing Situations at Work

Let's face it—everyone gets into embarrassing situations at work. And most usually, these are personal situations that flare up in a professional setting. Your fly is unzipped as you're giving a presentation. You e-mail a close friend about that lousy guy you're dating, and it gets broadcast to your entire internal mailing list. You have a fiery conversation about someone who drives you nuts, and that person is right outside the door. The list is endless.

Sadly, no universities offer courses on how to deal with embarrassing situations like these. Even your parents, for all their lessons and rules, didn't have much to say on the subject. So what to do? Use the perfect phrases that follow in this section of the book. They cover every situation you can imagine—and never wanted to! Of course, the nature of the embarrassing situation will be pivotal here.

● **Pretend it never happened.** This response is always helpful when the damage is minimal. Responding in any way, through a joke, an in-person apology, or a quick e-mail, may only cause people to remember something you wished they forgot. For example, Pat, a senior vice president of a technology firm, was giving a pep talk to his employees. In the middle of his talk, he emitted (and I'm embarrassed to say it) gas. Look, these things happen, right?

In this type of embarrassing situation, Pat could adopt the "pretend it never happened" approach. And who would really care? Difficult situation over.

● **Address the situation straight on.** If the embarrassing situation can diminish your credibility and reflect badly on you to your superiors, you must address it straight on. Soberly. Professionally. And immediately. Pat's situation was in no way egregious. But if a colleague overheard you commenting negatively on a client or ranting about a top-tier project, better take the most serious and direct route and ask for a meeting to discuss.

● **Send a heartfelt apology.** Personally, in the case of a colleague overhearing, I think this is the least desirable choice. I find the touchy-feely route more embarrassing than the situation that inspired it. If you ask me, workplace communications should remain just that—about actions, not emotions. But if that conversation your colleague overheard was about him or her—and could cause seriously hurt feelings—a simple apology won't be enough. Make it real. Specific. And hurry.

● **Make a joke.** This is the perfect way to diffuse a troubling bout of embarrassment. But only with the right audience. If Pat's team was composed of the humorous types (and they were), then they'd tease him eventually to his face or else joke about it behind his back. So Pat's way of handling it? He stopped, mid-sentence, and looked at the ceiling wonderingly. "Anyone heard a goose?" he asked. Everyone in the meeting laughed, and he went on with his ever-more energetic talk.

Here are more perfect phrases for situations you—or a dozen people you know—will confront at work.

A Personal E-Mail Reaches Someone Else

So maybe you're e-mailing a note to your babysitter and accidentally click on the wrong address. Not a problem. But if that e-mail is to your wife about your recent stomach problems, or worse, about your recent marriage strains, that's different. The plot thickens if it contains highly detailed information. Your best strategy is this: determine your relationship with the person who received it and the effect it might have on work. If it will affect your work life, you must address it. If doesn't . . . maybe not.

The Situation Contains Seriously Personal Information

You want a quick response from the person—to respect you and your privacy and keep the message under wraps. Start with a quick apology, and then ask for discretion.

● Sorry for sending you an e-mail intended for my ______. As you can see, things have been difficult, and I would really appreciate your keeping this to yourself.

● I just realized I accidentally cc'd you on my personal message—sorry. I would appreciate your helping me keep this difficult situation private.

●I apologize for sending you the e-mail intended for ____, and I appreciate your letting me know about it. Please keep the contents to yourself—I'm sure you understand why.

●Tom just told me that I accidentally sent you an e-mail I intended for ____. Sorry about the intrusion—as you can imagine it was for ____'s eyes only.

●I just realized I sent you an e-mail that I intended for ____. Sorry—your address was just above his in my address book, and I clicked on yours by mistake. This message is painful and private; would you mind deleting it, unopened?

The Situation Contains Mundane Information

You can take a lighter tone with this one—basically, you're trying to dissolve any ill will, no matter how slight, for cluttering up the person's mailbox. Add humor if you think your audience will respond to it.

●Sorry about sending that e-mail intended for my kid's babysitter. Now that I think of it—how about filling in if she can't make it (ha-ha)?

●Oops! Sorry to clutter up your mailbox. Didn't mean to send that last e-mail to you.

●Oh no______ told me I accidentally cc'd you on an e-mail. Sorry about that!

●Just learned about one of the many technology glitches to hit the workplace. This time, the fault is all mine. So sorry to have accidentally sent the e-mail to my kid's babysitter your way.

The Situation Incriminates Someone Else

Whatever you do, do not justify or explain why you sent the e-mail. Just make sure that the person understands that the message is not to be repeated and that you plan to resolve whatever difficulty you're in—and the person shouldn't try. This is especially significant if you're discussing a personal view about a professional situation.

●______ just told me that you received my e-mail about Francis. Please don't let Francis, or anyone else, know—okay? I'll discuss the matter privately with Francis soon.

●I just realized I sent you an e-mail intended for Eddy. Please disregard it—it's about a problem which I plan to resolve immediately.

●If you happened to get an e-mail from me with the subject line "________," please disregard it. I intended to send it to Eddy for his feedback before I moved forward.

●I just realized I accidentally sent you an e-mail intended for someone else. Please pay no attention—I was just venting.

Your Boss or Senior Official Accidentally Received the Message

Not only are you embarrassed, but you jeopardized your chances of being seen as a good employee. Good employees, after all, don't waste company time on personal messages. So you need to acknowledge the situation first, then explain it's a rare occurrence, and, finally, apologize for it.

●I just realized I accidentally cc'd you on an e-mail to ____. Please know that I rarely take work time for personal messages, but this situation was timely and I had little choice. Sorry that it happened.

●In reviewing my e-mails, I realized I accidentally sent you one intended for ______. I don't usually send personal messages at work unless they're necessary. I hope you understand, and I am sorry for the trouble.

●I learned that you mistakenly received my e-mail about ____. If you would like to discuss it with me, please let me know—I usually restrict my personal e-mails to my computer at home.

●You probably noticed my e-mail with the very unprofessional subject line "_____." I accidentally sent it your way. If the situation wasn't pressing, I would have waited until I got home to send it. Sorry, and please know that I spend the overwhelming majority of my work hours on professional matters.

Quick tip

Okay, you know that you shouldn't send personal messages from work. But face it: you spend most of your time at work, and now and then you can't help yourself. But remember: keep the messages as professional sounding as possible. Only state necessary information, and avoid discussing troubling or volatile thoughts and feelings. Here's an example:

Don't: At this point I think you're the biggest jerk I ever met. How dare you behave like that to me? Don't call. Don't e-mail. Get lost.

Do: Your behavior was unacceptable—I do not want further contact.

A Personal E-Mail Reaches Almost Everyone Else

A friend, who worked for a sensitive government agency, was madly in love with a man from a country with sensitive relations with the United States. After a relationship that was far stormier than the two nations' diplomatic relations, the pair broke up and he remarried. All was well until my friend realized she was at wits' end. She loved the guy. Craved him. So in a very undiplomatic gesture, she sent along an effusive love letter that just oozed with yearning. Little did she know, in his country everyone has access to everyone else's e-mails, and her private message was viewed by all in his company.

How you respond depends on the culture of the workplace, the severity (or embarrassment potential) of your message, and whether you incriminated the other person. Most likely, the message will go out to your cc list. And, most likely, other people will send it around. So someone will probably need to address it. In my friend's case, she didn't need to respond. Her ex-love interest did it for her, saying something like this: "Just to let you know—you shared your feelings with me and the entire workplace. I am happily married, but I, and everyone else here, wish you the best of luck."

Perfect Phrases When You're the Sender of the Message

The Message Reflects Poorly on the Intended Recipient

Start by apologizing for accidentally sending the e-mail. Then say whichever one of the following applies most:

- The message did not in any way reflect ____'s opinion.I have to apologize to him as well.
- Please know that the content reflects my point of view only.
- I alone am responsible for those opinions, and they do not reflect ___'s point of view.
- I expressed that point of view on impulse; it does not fully reflect my point of view or ____'s, in any way.

The Message Reflects Poorly on a Third Party

Once again, apologize first. Then say whichever one of the following applies most:

- The views were quite out of context and should not reflect poorly on anyone—especially _____.
- The viewpoints were entirely my own, and certainly others do not share it.
- If you have read the e-mail, please understand that the perspective is entirely my own and pertains to one circumstance only.
- Obviously, if you have any questions that resulted from this e-mail, you should probably clarify it with ____.

The Message Reflects Poorly on the Recipient's Workplace (Ouch!)

Apologize, and then put the message in context—immediately. And humbly. Especially if the recipient's job or some other aspect of work will be affected.

- As you know, I am not closely familiar with your workplace, so my opinions were inappropriate.
- _____ did not in any way influence my views of your office. You should ask her about her opinions—do not rely on my insights in any way.
- I did not mean to insult any of you—the feelings I expressed were out of context and entirely my own.

Quick tip

In this situation, you may want to invite the recipients to speak with you directly if they like.

Perfect Phrases When You're the Receiver of the Message

You can apply the phrases we discussed if you were sending the message and apply any of these strategies.

Humor

- Oops—none of you were suppose to see that e-mail. Sorry about that.
- For your eyes only, guys. So no telling, please.
- Just thought I'd share a personal message with all of my 100 closest personal friends (who happen to be on my cc list). My apologies.
- Pretend you never read this message. What message?

A Direct Approach

- Sorry about that message. ___ meant it for my eyes only.
- As you know, my situation is quite different from what _____ expresses. Sorry to catch you in the web.
- As you know, the e-mail was personal—sorry to open doors that should be closed at work!

You Send a Client a Proposal with a Different Client's Name in It

There are two things everyone in a business setting knows about proposals: (1) No one writes them from scratch. In fact, if people did, they'd never get any work done—or send more than two or three proposals a quarter. (2) Everyone acts as if his or her proposal were fresh, targeting that one, single, most remarkably valuable potential client. So if you accidentally put someone else's name in the "_____" slot, you're basically revealing a deep, dark secret . . . that everyone knows. Mostly, the mistake is embarrassing. And like most minor mistakes, it could cost you the potential client's goodwill. Of course, with the right message, it could also open doors to how great you are. Just rely on these perfect phrases.

Start by Acknowledging the Problem, So You Can Control How the Client Responds

- We just noticed we accidentally put a different company's name in your proposal.
- Oops—by mistake, we put someone else's name in the proposal.
- Our associate ______, whom you have been talking to about the project, just alerted us to the fact that another company's name is in the spot where yours belongs.
- Just wanted to let you know—somehow, _____'s name got into the proposal we wrote for you.

When You Think It's Appropriate, Apologize

- So sorry—I am really embarrassed about that mistake.
- I apologize—I don't know how that could have happened.
- Thanks for letting me know about the mistake. I feel pretty foolish!
- I'm so embarrassed about that mistake. Thanks for letting me know.
- Wow—what a mistake! My apologies.

When the Proposal Was Really Specific to Your Client

- We had an intern review the final cut—after our team developed it for you. Since we recently wrote a similar proposal, she probably got confused. Our apologies.
- As you probably know, we do cut and paste certain paragraphs discussing core services—but we designed the bulk of our proposal specifically for you.
- Somehow, one of our templates appeared in your proposal. Sorry about that.
- We borrowed information from a similar proposal. Somehow, the client's name ended up in the text.

When the Proposal Was Unique but the Name Was Not

Point out how the client's proposal was special, especially if you're providing more of something for the same price. Be specific about where this information resides.

- As you'll see on page 8 in our cost breakdown, we still provided 10 percent off all services.
- We will provide the additional services, at no additional expense, as we discussed. (See page 3, paragraph 4.)
- Because of our long relationship, we are giving you the Level 2 plan, without additional costs, as you can see in the "Details" section of the proposal.
- If you need more time to complete the project, we will be flexible. Normally, as you know, we add 10 percent to our fees, but in your case, we won't. You can find more specifics by contacting me or by looking at the cost breakdown in the last section of the proposal.

Quick tip

Most people flip through proposals quickly, looking for specific types of content—frequently cost. Then they move on. So it's possible that your reader may not read or otherwise notice the error. If so, then don't point it out. Just ignore the mistake and hope for the best. If the client does notice, then use the perfect phrases we just discussed.

Perfect Phrases for When You Notice the Mistake during a Presentation

Your response will depend on the audience. When possible, make a joke:

- Wow—look at that! When did you guys change your name?
- Hmmmm . . . are you really (other client's name here)? I know a company that has that name, too.
- How did that happen?
- Sorry about that . . . Embarrassed? Who's embarrassed?

Or address it with professional seriousness, as you would in an e-mail.

Here are two more examples:

● Pardon that mistake—we draft all our proposals for individual clients but occasionally lift a paragraph or two.

● That's the wrong name there—sorry.

Regardless, point the client to an advantage he or she alone has. Make sure that you point out the pertinent paragraph or line—this will ensure that the client remembers it and feels there is an advantage or special benefit:

● Just to remind you—if you look at page 3, we included all the provisions we discussed for your specific project.

● Bear with me for a moment, and turn to page 6. You can see I gave you all the discounts we discussed—I didn't want any of you to think this proposal was entirely canned.

Your Boss Overhears You Criticizing Something or Someone at Work

Oh boy. This is not what you wanted the boss to hear. But there you are, making a really bad impression on the person you least want to offend. So you better address the situation as soon as you can. Here are some phrases that will help when . . .

You Want to Introduce the Subject

● I think you may have overheard something I said, and I'd like to clear it up.

● I was wondering if we could talk for a minute about something I said yesterday.

● You may have heard me saying something rather stupid; can we talk about it?

● Do you have five minutes to address a problem I'm having? I know you heard me discuss it with ____ yesterday.

● I have had some concerns—I probably should have come to you directly, though. Do you have an opening in your schedule when we can talk?

You Want to Explain Your Comments

● Just so you know—I tend to vent now and then. So that conversation I was having yesterday with ___ was just my blowing off steam.

- I've been frustrated for some time and needed to talk it through.
- I wanted ____'s input about the best way to deal with the project. So I was discussing the problems—not all the things that are going right.
- My comments may have seemed highly critical, but in the final analysis, I think everything will work out quite well.
- I didn't think the issue was important enough to bring to you, but I did need to discuss it with someone at work.

You Were Speaking About a Specific Project

- I've worked on projects like this before and know it will turn out right. But first, I needed to address a few matters that are interfering with our progress.
- This project has had a unique set of circumstances, and it's been a challenge. To be sure, I am focused on doing it right.
- I know what it takes to get this project to be successful. But I needed input about the mistakes that continue to flare up.
- When I started this project, I hadn't anticipated these shortcomings. So I'm trying to find a way to address them.
- These problems are serious, but I'm still optimistic about the project.

You Were Speaking About a Fellow Employee

- I think ___ and I have personality issues. Since I have a hard time talking to her directly, I vent to other people.
- Even though I think that ___ and I have a difficult relationship, we can still work together productively.
- I understand that I'm not his manager, and I didn't feel comfortable bringing these issues to him directly.

That's why I was discussing them with ____.

- I want you to know that ____ likes ____. That's why I went to ____ with my frustrations. I knew she would be fair.
- Overall, I've had a good working relationship with ____. But from time to time, he really drives me crazy.

You Were (Yikes!) Speaking About Your Boss

- I realize that I should have brought these issues to you directly.
- I really enjoy working here and was complaining because I want to get clarity and feedback.
- I wasn't comfortable addressing these issues with you—although that probably would have been a better choice.
- I don't think these matters really amount to much—I just needed to get them off my chest.
- Please don't think I regularly complain like that—this one issue has been on my mind.

You Were Criticizing Someone, Then Realized the Person May Have Heard

Maybe you were talking and realized that person was right outside the door. Or maybe you thought you hung up the phone or that, during a conference call, the other person was long gone. Then guess what? There the person was . . . hanging on and on. It makes you want to shrink down to the size of a soda cracker. But wait—was the person really listening? Did he or she vanish without hanging up? Do you dare raise this embarrassing subject with the person? Or do you dare not? These perfect phrases will help you get through this king-size embarrassment.

When You're Not Sure Whether the Person Overheard

Obviously, keep your eyes open. If the subject of your discussion seems perfectly normal, don't worry about it. Your comments may have dissolved in the air. If that person ignores you or won't look you in the eye, take hold of the situation with the perfect phrases here. And act quickly—you don't want the ill will to fester.

- Is there anything you want to discuss with me?
- Do you have any concerns we should discuss?
- Are you doing okay? (Yes, something that simple can be a great opener.)
- Do you have any thoughts about our talk yesterday?
- Can I help you with anything?

When You Know the Person Overheard and You Want to Open Up the Discussion

- I'd really like to discuss what we were saying yesterday.
- I'm sure our comments were hurtful, but don't take them seriously.
- Let me know if you want to discuss what we were saying—we didn't mean anything by it.
- Sorry about what we were saying—you understand we were venting at the moment.
- We were tired from all the pressure and took it out on you. Sorry.
- You know how things can get out of hand, right? This was one of those times. Sorry.

When Your Comments Were Catty but Not Related to Work

Apologize. Not because you have to—but because you mean it. Insulting personal comments are nothing but destructive at work.

- So sorry about what we said—it was out of order.
- I feel bad about what we said. We didn't mean it.
- We never should have spoken about you that way. We were being jerks.
- I apologize for what we said. We were out of line.
- I feel embarrassed about what we said earlier. Please accept my apologies. It was wrong.

When Your Comments Were Related to the Person's Performance on the Job

When You Mean It

- I'm sorry you had to hear my thoughts this way. I think we should probably discuss them.
- I probably need to discuss these issues with the boss, instead of other employees.
- Sorry you had to hear about my perspective this way, but I really do think you need to look at some issues.

When You Don't Mean It

- Sorry—I was venting and took it out on you.
- This project has been making me crazy—it really isn't about you.
- After I left, I immediately regretted what I said.
- I don't feel that way—please don't take it for anything but venting.

Quick tip

It's useless to say that you shouldn't discuss other people at work. Of course you will. Everyone does. That's how you work out issues, get helpful insights, and let off the proverbial steam. But keep these two tips in mind: (1) There's work talk, and there's meanness. Don't be mean by making fun of a person's looks, mannerisms, or spouse. (2) Be discreet. Only tell people who will keep their mouths clamped shut and give you helpful and professional feedback. And . . . make sure you're having the discussion in private. This means not in the cafeteria where the wrong ears can overhear you, and not while standing around the water fountain—real or metaphorical. Find a quiet place at a discreet time and speak softly.

You Hear a Coworker Criticizing You

This situation is worse than embarrassing—it hurts. So you need to think carefully about why you want to approach the person you overheard. Do you want to explain your side of the story? Get more precise information about what your coworker said? Or perhaps you want to tell your coworker to stop chatting about you and put his or her energies to better use. The perfect phrases you'll find ahead will address each of these possibilities.

But before you apply them, ask yourself these additional questions: How does the conversation affect my work life? You don't want to overreact, nor do you want to miss an opportunity to glean helpful (albeit difficult) information about yourself. Also, what is the best venue for addressing the situation? If an e-mail—beware. These don't go away. If your response is too severe, it could be used against you. Finally, which of the participants in the conversation should you approach? The one most likely to be your ally? The leader of the gang?

Once you have a clear strategy, use these perfect phrases to get results when you want to . . .

Explain Your Side of the Story

Start by making your intentions clear, and then engage your coworker in a conversation. Make sure that you don't sound overly defensive—a hard thing to do when you're inwardly fuming. Be specific about what you overheard, when appropriate.

- I overheard you and _____ discussing your views on my contribution to the project. I'd like to explain why I took the approach I did so you're clear about my motivations and what I believe will be the outcome.
- I understand that you have some reservations about my contributions to the _____. I'd like to discuss this issue with you so you're clear about my direction.
- Since you and I work together every day, I think we should discuss my work style so you have a better sense of what to expect from me and why. I am aware that you have some reservations.
- I think we need to talk about my contributions to the _____ so far. You may not be aware of my motivations, and I want to be sure we're able to work together as productively as possible.

Quick tip

Steer clear of strong language that could alienate the person you're speaking to or create an even more adversarial relationship. Remember, you're trying to put an end to the situation, not fuel it.

Do Not

- What you're doing is spreading lies, and you better shut up about it.
- You've been saying some really rude things about me.

Do

- I understand you have reservations . . .
- I want to get clarity and put an end to any discord.

Sending an e-mail? Rude or overly emotional language could be construed as harassment and will work against you.

Get Precise Information About What Was Said

Try giving the other person an opportunity to discuss the issue with you—this may or may not work. But remember, you can't force that person.

- When you were in that meeting with _____, I overheard my name mentioned. Do you have something you'd like to discuss with me?
- I heard you speaking with _____, and your tone didn't seem too happy. I'd like to know more about what you're thinking so we can settle any differences that may be hovering.
- I realized that you and _____ may be harboring some resentment. I'd like to know what the problem is so we can address it.
- If you have any problems with me, I'd like to hear them directly. Otherwise, they won't get any better.
- Since we work together every day, we should discuss differences directly. I overheard you and ____ talking. It would be helpful for you to tell me what you think.

Get a Coworker to Stop Talking

If you overheard a coworker saying rude, inappropriate, or otherwise disparaging comments, it's best to send an e-mail. That way you have a paper trail. If you opt to speak directly, send a follow-up e-mail covering what you said. Regardless, be specific when possible, including dates and individual comments. If someone alerted you to these comments, mention this in your e-mail, as well. The following perfect phrases will serve as great talk stoppers:

- I overheard you and _____ talking about me in the cafeteria yesterday. At that time, you said that I was _____ and _____. While I did not wait to hear the remainder of the conversation, I want to remind you that these comments are personal and mean-spirited and inappropriate at work.
- Several people have alerted me to the fact that you've been making disparaging remarks about my _____ and _____. This is inappropriate for the workplace and diminishes my reputation. If you have grievances about my professional performance, please tell me directly.

  If you have issues about me personally, please keep them to yourself.
- Several times this week, you have been making jokes at my expense, most

notably at the ____ and ____. This is counterproductive and divisive. You need to stop this at once.

You Demand Payment from a Client Who, It Turns Out, Paid You Already

If you own a small business and are consumed with cash flow issues, this embarrassment is probably far more common than you want to admit. Of course, even if you work for a large business, cash flow issues reign supreme. You bill and bill and bill and wait and wait . . . and get promises that the check . . . is . . . almost . . . in . . . the . . . mail. Finally, frustrated, you send an angry e-mail. But face it, the client deserves it, right? Only to realize that envelope tucked in your box has the client's return address and contains a check. Or even worse, your bookkeeper deposited the check a week before but neglected to tell you. Try one of the following.

When the Payment Just Arrived

If the check is really late, thank the client without letting him or her off the hook:

- We just received the payment I discussed in my e-mail and have noted this in our records.
- Fortunately, the payment arrived shortly after I sent you the e-mail. We will deposit it immediately.
- The payment arrived in our office shortly after my e-mail stating it was three weeks late.
- Our office received your payment for services we provided on June 5. As you know, you still have outstanding bills for June 10 and June 15.

When the Payment Arrived a Week or Two Before

In this case, you can apologize. True the client was late—but not as late as you thought. On the other hand, a polite thank you can help smooth any residue ridges and create a faster cash flow in the future:

● Our bookkeeper just informed us that we received the check on June 1. Thank you for sending it.

● According to our records, we actually received the payment we e-mailed you about earlier two weeks ago. We apologize for our alarming message.

● After sending you the e-mail about our overdue payment, we discovered that you sent it on May 19. Thank you for your attention, and we apologize for any disturbance our previous messages may have caused.

● We received the payment—due date May 19—on June 1. So your account is settled. We apologize for our most recent e-mails.

When the Billing System Was Wrong and You Never Provided the Service

Apologize? Definitely. And be quick (and humble) about it:

● I just noted a mistake in our billing system. We have been billing you for a service we didn't provide. I am so sorry about the mistake and any confusion that caused on your end.

● Please accept our apologies. In reviewing our accounts, we realized that we have billed you for a service we didn't provide. We have corrected this error in our system and apologize again.

If Possible, Make a Joke About It

● We just discovered we never provided the service listed on our invoice B–202. Well, that explains why you never paid us! Please accept our apologies.

● Oops—we just recognized a glitch in our billing. We were hounding you for a payment you don't owe. So sorry!

Please forgive the disturbance. Of course, if you want to send us the money anyway . . .

You Emphasize a Point—Strongly and in Front of Lots of People—Then Immediately Discover You're Wrong

This situation offers several layers of embarrassment. The least embarrassing is when you make a mistake in a meeting of colleagues and (we hope) friends,

and someone immediately corrects you. Worse is when you are speaking as an authority at a meeting and someone contradicts your wisdom—and you realize the person is correct. Even worse, and the most embarrassing, is when you're giving a talk in an ultra-packed room. During the Q&A's, one of the participants corrects you about a point you mentioned earlier. Several others in the room (audibly) agree with the participant. Now what? If you're lucky, you'll have these perfect phrases handy.

When Someone Corrects You in a Small-Group Setting—Whether a Chat Room, a Series of Cc'd E-Mails, or a Face-to-Face Meeting

Say thank you, and see if the person can provide information that will help you in the future. This will help you regain control and prove that you are the ultimate professional.

- Thanks for that correction. Do you know where I can go to learn more?
- That's helpful, actually. Who is your source for this?
- Thanks for pointing that out. That changes things.
- This will help me clarify my position as we move on.
- I didn't realize that. Thanks for letting me know.

When Someone Corrects You When You're an Authority

Regain control by agreeing with the correction whole-heartedly. Appreciatively. And above all, sincerely. Then keep the conversation (or chat room comments, blogs, or e-mails) flowing.

- You're absolutely right. Thank you for that correction.
- Now that you mention it, yes, you're quite right. I appreciate your input. Now let's move to the next point.
- Good insight. Let's see how that affects the next point.
- Thanks for correcting me on that point. Now let's discuss . . .
- In his comments on my blog, ____ correctly pointed out that . . .
- ____'s point, as published in your journal, that ___ should have been ___, was correct. I appreciate that feedback. However, the conclusion remains the same, for these reasons . . .

Among Colleagues

If you have a close working relationship, and go to each other's weddings and Fourth of July parties, then you can take a distinctly personal approach. Where appropriate, add a touch of humor to dilute any tension.

- Sorry guys—he's right.
- Wow—You're right. Why didn't I know that.
- Actually, ___ is right again. So let's move on.
- Good point. Really good point. (Simple is fine.)

Among Clients

Try to accept the correction without losing your credibility by highlighting the legitimacy of your point or the ultimate value of your contribution:

- I appreciate the insights ___ provided in his e-mail earlier today. Please know that the change does not affect our outcome.
- ___ rightfully pointed out that _____. Fortunately, this means you actually get more of the _____ we provide.
- While ___ certainly raises an important point, most professionals agree that my original figure is also applicable.
- I have inputted the changes ___ made in our analysis and am sending along the revision.

You Provide Facts or Advice in a Report That Proves to Be Wrong

What a misery. You write a report. You give it to the client, your team, or your boss. This is a definitive statement of what needs to happen next, and the outcome depends on your opinions. All is well until your prediction, facts, or who knows what else turns out to be false. Embarrassing? No kidding. So start by acknowledging the mistake and, where appropriate, thanking the person for telling you about it, using these perfect phrases:

- Sorry about the inaccuracy in that report.
- Thank you for letting me know about the problem with that report. I am embarrassed and perplexed about how that could happen.

● I appreciate your contacting me immediately about the misinformation in the report.

● I checked the report several times, as did the others on the team. So I was really surprised and embarrassed by the mistake.

● I apologize for the incorrect information in the report. I was really diligent in double-checking the information and getting feedback from others when I had questions.

Then redeem yourself by offering something to compensate for the mistake. Make sure what your offer is equal to the damage you caused. So if the mistake cost a client money or time, try to provide a service at no cost. If the report was for your boss or internal client, demonstrate how you checked your methodology to ensure the mistake won't happen again. Regardless, correct that mistake when possible.

Here are some perfect phrases when settling up with . . .

The Boss

● I'll go back and check the report again and e-mail you a new version on Monday.

● I'll get the team together, and we'll review the report again after work today.

● I will go through my process when compiling the report to determine where I went wrong and avoid a repeat in the future.

● Please know that I strive for accuracy and double-check my facts. I will determine where I went wrong and get back to you immediately.

A Client

● We are embarrassed about the error in our report. We will send you a revision promptly and provide support for the remaining implementation process at no additional charge to you.

● In your e-mail, you requested 10 extra ____ as compensation for the problems. We will gladly provide 15.

● We have reviewed the report closely and will get you a revision first thing on Monday. We will also give you an additional month of our services at no extra expense to you.

● Just to assure you: problems of this rarely occur. In fact,

I don't know of another occasion. I would like to meet with you and anyone else from your company to review the corrections and see how we can reconcile this problem moving forward.

Your Coworkers

● I'll review the report again and e-mail all of you a revised copy.

● I'll be happy to correct the other reports to reflect the changes and will send you a copy—on Friday at the latest.

● Sorry about this guys. Just let me know how I can help as we move forward.

● As you know, I've been diligent about checking facts. If anyone has insights about how I could have done this better, I would be most appreciative.

Sometimes, of course, when the mistake wasn't too severe and really just embarrassing, apologize and move on:

● Thanks for pointing out the problem on page 6. I corrected it.

● I appreciate your feedback. Thanks.

● I don't know how that incorrect number got in there. Thanks for pointing it out.

● Many thanks for the correction.

Quick tip

Apologizing is a delicate balance between letting a person know you feel bad about a mistake and treating an ordinary error as a catastrophe. So be careful of overapologizing. You may call more attention to the problem than necessary. Even worse, in some professions, you may even invite a lawsuit. For example, a truck driver at a company where I consult hit a car accidentally while backing out of an alley. No one was killed, fortunately, but two of the passengers were injured and the car was totaled.

The company received bad press in the local newspapers. Rather than apologize briefly and assure the public that all its drivers were required to attend classes on safe driving skills, the company went on and on and on . . . about the mental and physical pain the passengers must have felt and how heartsick it (as a sensitive company) felt about the issue. This public admission of fault cost the company quite a considerable amount in court.

You Accidentally—but Obviously—Burp,Groan, or Break Wind (It Does Happen)

The workplace is about being professional, discreet, and overall, nonhuman. Face it: we have rules of delicacy for everything we do. Rather than gulp down a soda when we've been dying of thirst, we sip it slowly and carefully. Rather than belch, which would feel soooo good, we clamp our lips shut and hold in any unseemly emissions. As for clothes: men wear suits in the blazing heat of summer, and women wear suits or dresses with obligatory sleeves. Should a sweat stain mark the garment, especially beneath the armpits . . . how embarrassing!

Okay, let's be reasonable, please. These situations shouldn't be embarrassing any more than breathing should be embarrassing, but there you go. So trust these quick and effective perfect phrases to clean up the mess in these situations.

Situation: You Have Just Broken Wind or Know You're About To

These perfect phrases are especially perfect if you're a guy among a group of guys with a great working relationship. These are usually not recommended for mixed company.

- Everyone out! For your own safety! I'm about to let loose.
- Phew. That's disgusting. Did I just do that? Sorry folks.
- Wow! That's a bummer.
- Open the windows! Close your doors!

But remember, this response only works with audiences with that special adolescent sense of humor. Otherwise, go for a more serious and sincere approach:

- Sorry, I've had an upset stomach these days.
- My apologies. What a thing to have happen!
- Sorry guys—I couldn't help it.
- Excuse me.

Situation: You Belch Loudly in Front of a Mixed Crowd

This one is far less offensive, as it disturbs the ears only. So a quick apology will do:

- Sorry, folks.
- Pardon me.
- I beg your pardon.
- Excuse me.
- Yikes—sorry about that.

Situation: You Notice That Your Fly Is Unzipped, Especially in Front of a Crowd When You're the Speaker

Imagine a lecturer at college who was hilarious and wonderful and addressed a least 500 students at a time. And guess what? He spent 90 minutes lecturing with his fly down. What's the best way to handle?

You Can Tell a Joke

- Just getting a little air conditioning.
- Just letting the breeze get in.
- Excuse me—guess I was thinking about this talk when I got dressed today. From now on, I'll pay better attention.

Or Apologize Sincerely

- Pardon me . . .
- Excuse me, would you (turn and zip) . . .

Or If You Learn About the Situation Later

You can tie it into a talk the next time you meet to add levity and regain control of the situation. Here are some sample phrases—the actual ones you use should depend on the content of your discussion:

- We must pay attention to details—like, say, unzipped flies.
- Let's make sure the proposal looks fully professional—like an unzipped fly, it will only embarrass us.
- Of course, we're always ready to forgive unwitting indiscretions like, say, an unzipped fly.

Situation: You Have Stains Under Your Arms When Leading a Meeting or during a Presentation

You Can Be Direct

- Seems like the heat is hurting my clothes.
- Pardon my appearance—I know it's not the latest in fashion.

Or Indirect—They'll Get What You Mean

- I sure am hot—are you?
- Boy, is it warm in here!

Or Say Nothing

Quick tip

In mentioning an embarrassing situation after the event, make sure the recipient will have noticed and remembered it. Otherwise, say nothing.

You Call a Person by the Wrong Name

Like so many embarrassing situations, this one doesn't mean a whole lot. No one is hurt. No insult is intended. And life, basically, goes on unchanged. Only the way people respond, you'd never know it! They act like the wrong name—or worse, the wrong pronunciation of their name—is a kick in the face. How dare you! And spell the name wrong? You may as well have publicly humiliated them. So you need to put a few verbal bandages on the sore—with the right perfect phrases, they'll heal in more ways than you think.

When Calling Someone by the Wrong Name in a Meeting or in Introducing Him or Her to a Colleague

- Sorry, you must remind me of someone with that name.
- Yes, of course. Sorry I forgot.
- You remind me of a ______.

● I'm really bad with names, but I remember your face and our previous conversation perfectly.

● Sorry—that's what I meant to say.

● Thanks. I don't know why I got confused.

When Spelling the Name Incorrectly in an E-Mail

● My apologies—I should have known.

● Sorry about incorrectly spelling your name.

● Thanks for correcting my spelling.

● Thanks for the correction. I know someone with your name who spells it differently.

● Thanks for letting me know—I'll spell it correctly from here on in!

When Someone Points Out That You Misspelled a Name in a White Paper, Newsletter, or Blog

● Thank you for catching that problem: As you can see, I have corrected it on my blog.

● I appreciate your calling my attention to that mistake.

● Thanks for letting me know. Amazing how details get away from me.

Mention the mistake—and the correction—in the next publication:

● We accidentally spelled the mayor's name incorrectly in our blog. It should be ________.

● In our summer 2008 newsletter, we incorrectly spelled the advisor's name. It should be _______.

● The name of the ambassador from 1990 to 1996 should have been ______. We will make that correction in future commentaries and publications.

When Mispronouncing Someone's Name

● Can you say the correct pronunciation again, so I'm sure to get it right this time? (Repeat the correct pronunciation.)

● Sorry. Did you say _______? (Repeat the correct pronunciation.)

● I had no idea. Thank you for telling me.

- (Repeat the name.) Is that correct? Thank you.

When You're Unsure of How to Pronounce Someone's Name—Ask

Better safe than sorry, as the expression goes. Besides, asking for the correct pronunciation of a person's name shows respect, courtesy, and care.

- Could you tell me how to correctly pronounce your name?
- So I get your name right, how do you pronounce it?
- Is this the correct pronunciation of your name: _______
- How do you say your name? I want to be accurate.

第三章

聚光灯下（怎么会站在这儿?！）

这样的事总是难免。比如你正好好地干着自己的事，突然接到电话——你的一位同事腿骨折了，你必须代替对方出席会议。或者你正准备开始讲话时却发现把幻灯片忘在了千里之外的办公室。你已经在众目睽睽之下了，无处藏身。在使自己出洋相或是使公司失望、蒙羞之前，请牢记以下要点，然后使用“完美措辞”帮你摆脱困境。不管聚光灯有多耀眼，这都会有效。

- **不要急，给自己一点时间。**有时情况的确很紧急（比如开讲前发现忘带幻灯片），但不要急于行动，给自己一点时间制定策略以应对局面。承认自己忘带了？谎称航空公司给弄丢了？还是假装根本没打算用幻灯片并就此开始？

- **保持镇定。**无论在什么情况下都不要显得坐立不安，不要大声叹息或者抓耳挠腮，这些都会暴露你的尴尬。相反，要挺起胸，与观众目光交流时保持微笑。如果你必须做点什么来缓解紧张的话，那就做点有益的事，比如整理一下讲稿，或者在活动挂图上准备一页新内容。

- **不要过度道歉。**这将使人关注到你的过失，而这是最要不得的。所以，如果当时情形确实需要道歉的话，简短说声“对不起”即可。记住，任何人都会犯错误，或者是在别人需要时无法提供必要的信息。所以，尽最大努力去做吧，要自信并努力去控制局面。还要切记不能手足无措（见上述第二点）。

- **求教于另一位专家。**比如有人问你一个问题而你不知该如何回答。

毕竟这是你的发言主题，你应该知道答案，不是吗？在这种情况下，尽你所能去回答并且建议提问者去向其他人请教。更好的做法是事后找到答案，发电子邮件或打电话给予答复。这可以表明你很专业并且很热心。如果是新闻界打电话询问一件棘手的事，最好是请一位新闻发言人回复（他/她会以正确的方式给出正确的答案）。

- **继续进行，不要停顿。**不管是忘带幻灯片、讲义不够发，还是无法回答记者的问题而将其推给别人，都不要紧，一定不能中断。打电话给你们公司的发言人，确保他/她与你的同事取得联系（就算是面对有敌意的提问也要如此）。这样做可以表明你是在采取合作的态度，而且没什么可隐瞒的。如果是忘带讲义或幻灯片的话，可以记下参加者的姓名和地址，过后给他们发一份。根据发布会的性质不同，有时这种情况甚至可以成为一个良好的商业机会。给参加者发简介或者名片，并且叮嘱他们有事可以给你打电话。

大庭广众之下感到难以胜任，毫无准备

这种情况时常会发生，就算你的确是一位十足的专业人士、业内专家或者是一个真正的佼佼者也不例外。进门时你还在想着是给一群（初出茅庐的）新员工讲话，结果却发现要面对的是一群年长的、资深的副总裁们。或者由于别人都一无所知，而你了解一些皮毛，所以就选你做报告。就这样你站在了白板前、讲台上或者是网络摄像头前，天知道有多少探询的目光正注视着你。该怎么办呢？

当你开始冒汗时，要冷静下来，闭上嘴默念以下完美措辞。

- 我能行。我成功搞定过比这更难的事情。
- 我对讲话内容了解透彻。我所说的都是有用的。
- 我必须相信自己，尽力去做，这就是我要做的。
- 不管怎样，这将是一次宝贵的经历。
- 人们通常都喜欢我的讲话，所以这些人很可能也会喜欢的。
- 有助于应对这个场面的三件事？（然后自问自答，可以这样开始：

“喝点水”，“在开场白里问问他们想听些什么”。）

小提示

记住，不要坐立不安或者大惊小怪。要昂首挺胸、信心十足。

划定你的主题

你得掌控住会议内容，这很重要。所以要明确你的讲话重点，要突出哪些方面或忽略哪些方面。如果确有必要做出取舍而你又准备了幻灯片的话，那你可能就需要跳过一两页或者是对某些内容一带而过。一定要确保自己的讲话方向和领域是自己能驾驭自如的。

在介绍内容时，一定要告诉听众你要讲的内容以及他们将如何从中获益。

- 今天我们将回顾七项主要原则，这些内容有助于你们采用新的模式来促进业务增长。
- 今天的讲座中我们将继续论述……所以你们可以……
- 今天我们将讲述……由此你们可以得到三个结果。
- 今天我所讲的内容已经帮助了很多情况与你们相似的部门取得了如下成功业绩。
- 采用今天我所介绍的策略，你们将能够取得……
- 本次会议你们将获得全新的信息，你们的竞争对手还完全没有涉猎。

要特别强调你所提供的信息的可信性，并且最好能够引导听众的预期。

错误用语：

- 你们学到的东西将有助于你们的机构做得更好。
- 本次讲座的内容将会是富有成效的。

正确用语：

- 我所讲的七种策略将有助于你们在目前的低迷时期增加利润。
- 本讲座中所讲述的策略来自于三位有影响的业界领袖，采用这些策略可以让你们在一年之内取得 25% 的增长。

制定规则

你能容许听众的提问打断你的讲话吗？还是更乐于在讲完之后回答？也许听众所在的公司有自己的偏好，但是不要紧，你可以制定自己的规则，这将树立你的威信并且有助于控制局面。

- 请把你们的问题留到讲座结尾时。
- 如果有问题的话请先等一下，我将在适于暂停的时候回答问题。
- 我将在休息之前回答问题。
- 在讲座过程中可以随时提问。
- 如果有问题的话请举手，我会在讲完这一点时叫你。

当你不知道答案时（无论是该问题与讲座无关，还是你本人就是不会）

- 此问题我随后答复你。
- 这个问题超出了我的专业范围，我会去查找答案再答复你。
- 这个问题很好，我过会儿回答。（在休息时找到答案。）
- 这是个很好的问题，但是与今天所讲主题没有直接关系，时间有限，我现在不能回答，抱歉。
- 这个问题需要细致全面的解答，目前我还没有做好充分的准备。

没带必要的幻灯片、讲义或者是演讲稿的复印件

人们参加发布会总是期望得到点什么：一本书、讲义、工作表或者是内部报告，等等。谁知道呢？也许有人会随手扔进垃圾桶，也可能有人会在空白处一丝不苟地做笔记，并且一直保留到退休。不论哪种情况，他们都希望得到这些材料。如果你没有准备的话，他们会觉得自己受骗了。更糟的是，在整个讲座过程中无论你表现得多优秀，他们都将心情

不佳。以下提供一些措施，运用完美措辞来弥补此遗憾。

致歉

你总得说点什么对吧？一句简短的致歉可以表达你的真诚。不过也别过了头，可以使用以下这些简短而友好的完美措辞。

- 很抱歉，今天我没带讲义。
- 今天我的报告不用幻灯片，请原谅。
- 对不起，我没带讲义。
- 我们可以看一些例子，我将把它们写在白板上。很抱歉今天没带工作表。
- 我为今天的报告准备了一些辅助材料，但是很抱歉忘记带来了。

不要使用以下语句，它们会把你的错误放到聚光灯下。

不要说	例句
我忘了……	该死！我忘了带工作表了！
难以置信……	难以置信我竟然会这样做（竟然没有这样做）！
哎呀！	哎呀！我真是糊涂透顶了！ 哎呀！我一定是太累了！ 哎呀！我今天真是太蠢了！
肯定是因为……	肯定是因为我实在累坏了！ 肯定是因为我太忙了！ 肯定是因为我的助手不在，而我又不善于处理细节。
我总是（从不）这样。	我从来没这样过。 我总是这样。 长途旅行时我总是这样。

致歉的同时做出解释

如果不是你的个人原因，同时理由很充分、很有趣的话，那不妨讲给大家听。若并非如此，还是不说为妙。完美措辞的具体运用取决于当时的具体情况，以下这些例句会有所帮助。

- 讲义装在我的一个行李箱里，航空公司一直没有送到，但愿我能很快收到。
- 我出发的前一天办公室关门了，我没法拿到这些材料。
- 我的公文包在机场被偷了（教科书里最老套的借口，但是如果情况确实如此也不妨实话实说）。

承诺稍后补送材料（甚至还会提供额外的材料）

为了消除影响（不管影响是多么的轻微），要向对方承诺一定会发送讲义和 PPT。简单、直接地对他们说你会发给他们，而不要用征询的语气，这样你就能掌控局面并且不给他们拒绝的机会。

不要征询对方的意愿

- 如果你们愿意的话，我可以在下周给你们发讲义。
- 是否需要我把这些 PPT 发给你们?
- 如果你们想要复本的话，只要在会后把电子邮箱留给我就行了。
- 如果你们还是想要复本的话，可以把电子邮箱或者通讯地址留给我，我随后发给你们。

要直接做出承诺

- 我下周的第一件事就是给你们发送讲义。
- 我会马上给你们发送这些 PPT。
- 会后把你们的电子邮箱留给我，我会把复本发给你们。
- 把你们的电子邮箱和通讯地址留给我，我马上把复本发给你们。

可能的话向听众解释会后收到的这些材料的价值

- 你们将在周五收到工作表，可以试着做几个例题，这样就能够检验一下自己记住了多少，并且便于你们在实际工作中应用这些知识。
- 我将用电子邮件把 PPT 发给你们，你们可以将其加入到自己的笔记里。
- 我会马上把案例研究部分发给你们，你们可以将它们与自己的实际工作情况进行比较。

一定不要使用消极的词语，否则将有碍于你后续的行动。

消极用语	例句
最不济……	最不济我也可以用电子邮件把 PPT 发给你们。
不幸的是……	不幸的是，我只能晚些时候用电子邮件把案例研究部分发给你们了。
抱歉……	抱歉，下周回来时我才能发给你们。
直到……时才能……	直到下周我才能把它们发给你们。

可能的话再发送一些额外的材料（尽量创造机会这样做）。这不会让你有额外的支出，却能够取得对方的好感。

告诉听众你所发放材料的内容以及它的价值所在。

● 我还会附送一系列的案例研究，这将有助于你们把相关内容应用到更多的场合中。

● 我将送给你们一本我写的书，以便于你们了解公关部门是如何帮助你们加强客户服务的。

● 除此之外，你们还将收到一份 PPT。它提供了今天讲座内容的背景知识。

顺便说一句，你也不必太直白，只要使对方印象深刻即可。当然，具体措辞取决于你发送的材料，以下是一些例句：

● 你们还将收到一份我公司总裁在安全委员会发言的讲话稿，该讲话得到了《纽约时报》商务版的好评。

● 我将送给你们一盘录像带，名为《正确了解自我：自我激励的 10 条策略》。超过 4 万人使用这些知识改善了自己的生活并且创造了财富。

回访

回访的必要性有很多，其中之一是要确认对方收到了你的材料。谁知道呢？也许会意外地被邮件过滤器过滤掉，或者是被意外删除，所以最好是确认一下。而且你也希望听众能记得你，并给你一个较高的评价。这还将带来另外一个好处：他们有可能会雇用你。但是要当心，要使你的回访显得是一次真诚的询问，而不是一次推销宣传。

电话回访用语

提醒对方你的身份：

- 上周我在……做了关于……的报告。
- 我是……的销售代表。
- 我是……研讨会的发言者。

告诉对方你为其发送的材料。

- 我想确认一下您是否收到了我发送的材料，包括我当初承诺的幻灯片以及额外的一支金笔。
- 只是想确认一下您是否收到了我周四发出的电子邮件，邮件内容是我的一些工作表。
- 请问您是否收到了我的邮件，是关于上周三……的讲座。

电子邮件回访用语

对方可以从电子邮件的标题和发件地址了解到你的身份，所以只需提醒对方你讲座的内容即可，并且询问对方是否收到了相关材料。

- 希望您对亚特兰大会议感到满意，并且希望您已经收到了关于我的……主题讲座的讲义。
- 上周的专题讲座后，您一切都还顺利吧！您收到我周三发出的工作表了吗？
- 仅此通知您关于我周五……讲座的案例研究已经发给您了，收到后请通知我。

需要延长会议或者通过电子邮件重新召集会议讨论某个棘手的问题

这种事发生的频率超过你的想象：与会者开始坐立不安，你已经没有时间了，可是还得继续开会。在这种情况下不能强迫大家留下，但是可以说服他们。还有些情况是你需要提早结束会议，同时又必须发个电子邮件把大家重新召集起来。无论哪种情况，以下这些完美措辞都有助于你尽量争取到时间。

当意识到自己要延时

告诉大家具体的时间安排，使其有思想准备，并且解释需要他们留下来的原因。可能的话强调一下积极的因素（尤其是诸如争论、不满甚至愤怒等此类负面情绪可能会蔓延开）。告诉大家你计划取得的成果，以及这种安排最终有利于大家的原因。

- 我们只剩10分钟了，但是我仍然有两点重要内容要讲，希望大家不要错过。所以我们要在整点以后再延长15分钟，然后再休息。
- 请先别收起笔记本，我们需要再延长10分钟，这样每人都将明确自己的职责，项目才能顺利进展。
- 让我们再延长5分钟吧，这样我就能回答所有的问题了。
- 我们延长到九点半吧，以便讲完________和________刚刚提到的所有重要问题，回顾这些内容对每个人都有益处。
- 我们散会前必须解决好这些预算问题，以便该项目能最终获得启动，所以我们准备延长到12点。
- 为了最终达成一致的计划，我们打算再延长20分钟左右。

小提示

对那些确实需要离开的人灵活处理，但是要确保他们能够获得自己错过的信息。

- 如果有谁与客户约好了，那我能理解你们必须离开，但是请确保你们能从同事那里获得笔记。
- 那些要乘坐下午3点班车的人可以按时离开，谁能给他们提供一下笔记？
- 如果谁有更重要的会议，请自便，但是要找人给你们提供会议记录。
- 如果有谁必须离开的话，请拿到我们下周的目标列表，不管怎样每人都将负有自己的职责。
- 我们将在会议结束时分配任务，如果有谁必须离开的话，我能够理解，但是我们仍将为其分配任务。

已经超过了时限，但你仍然希望大家能留下来

关注时限和目的

时限 **目的**

● 大家能再等 10 分钟吗？我们要做一个重要的决定。

● 我们只需要大约 10 分钟，而且你们对此方案的建议将是至关重要的。

● 大家先别急，在散会之前我还需要大约 10 分钟左右做出结论。

● 我们还不能散会，至少还需要 15 分钟，不然的话我们就没有动力了。

需要另找时间完成此议题

要明确再次开会的时间，或者明确你采用何种方式与大家联系取得决议。

错误用语：

● 我们并没有完成全部内容，还需要再次开会。

● 有人会再与你们联系，确定合适的时间来完成这些事宜。

● 我们将于近期再次开会，并且完成这些讨论。

正确用语：

● 我们需要更多的时间来解决所有的问题，请于下周确定一个共同的时间和地点。

● 我们必须完成目标列表。________，能否请你在明天与大家联系一下确定最佳时间？

● 下周一我们必须做好这份预算，本周五上午把你们自己方便的时间告知我，我来安排一下。

● 明天告诉________你们下周四是否方便参会，如果不行的话我们就周五开会，不能再晚了。

● 周四下午两点我们再次开会，如果有谁不方便的话请通知我，但是无法改期，你可能会失去投票的机会。

通过电子邮件重新召集会议

提醒参会者上次会议的内容、你要完成的日程以及开会的时间。

● 由于5月14日的会议超时了，我们没能确定项目预算，所以我们将于5月21日下午3点在________会议室再次召开会议。

● 全体会议的目的是要为……确定实施策略。我们已经有了一些好的想法，但仍需要制定具体的策略。请告知________你们下周何时方便。

● 5月19日的会议中我们决定将最终方案提交给________，为了信守我们的计划，需要在周二再开一次会。

● 如你们所知，我们上周二的会超时了。为了决定下一步的行动并使项目走上正轨，我们必须在本周二再次开会。

小提示

使用积极的语言，专注于那些将要取得的目标而不是那些未完成的事项。这样可以带来乐观的情绪，尤其是在人们感到不满或不悦时，这样做尤为重要。要注意一些微妙但却重要的区别。

错误用语：

● 我们还没有完成预算分配。

● 我们根本还未阐明那些情况下应采取的正确步骤。

● 玛丽提的最后一个问题还没有得到解决。

正确用语：

● 我们需要完成预算分配。

● 我们必须阐明那些情况下应采取的正确程序。

● 应该回答一下玛丽提出的最后一个问题。

同事让你处理某一难题，并且你知道与会者不喜欢这一话题

俗话说：总得有人啃骨头。为什么你不能去做呢？当然你能想出众多理由拒绝这么做，比如说你没有资格、情况太复杂或是你不喜欢争吵。你已经够头疼了，不是吗？但是既然你已经处于这样的境地，那就既来之则安之吧。每个人都会遇到这种情况的。以下这些完美措辞可以帮助你冷静下来，而且还能帮你处理其他一些紧张局面。

通过电子邮件处理有争议的问题

当处理一些棘手问题时最好是面谈，这样你可以看到对方的反应，并且根据他们的感受来组织你的语言。比如说如果对方显得担忧，你就可以想办法使其放松一下，可以做个评论、微笑一下或者显出同情的样子。采用书面方式时就无法这样做了，读者可能会愤怒地尖叫或是凄然地点头，你都无从得知。所以，你最好的选择就是询问他们何时方便面谈。以下这些完美措辞会有所帮助。

标题行

标题行要简短并且能表达足够的信息，应该尽量引起收信者的注意并促使其打开邮件阅读。但是，不要引起对方的恐惧。可能的话使用一些说服力强的动词，并且持积极向上的态度，或者就只是要求一次会面。

- ________项目变更
- 我们周一可以见一次面吗？
- ________的最新资讯
- ________的新动向
- 计划变更，可以和您讨论一下吗？
- 开会讨论发展问题，周四可以吗？

首行

这一行将决定整个邮件的基调，不要显得太忧郁，也不要显得危言耸听。记住，你需要使对方保持信心，这样他们才能以最冷静、最有效的方式做出回应。

- 我们刚刚获知________项目有了一些变动，需要和您一起讨论一下。
- 我希望下周能早点与您会面，讨论一些近期发生的关于预算方面的事务。
- 我们刚刚收集到一些关于________项目的重要信息。
- 为了……我们需要调整一下时间安排。
- 今天早些时候________来电话说他有一些重要信息，他认为我应该和您讨论一下这些信息。

主体

加入任何能有所帮助的信息，但是不要太多。你的任务就是使对方能尽快与你面谈，所以内容要点到为止，不要罗列大量对方不感兴趣的信息。要确保收件人明确其在会谈中所处的地位。

- ________已经在此项目的多个方面改变了主意，我们需要讨论一下下一步该怎么办。
- 拨款方面发生了一些变化，我可以详细地给你讲一下。
- 我们需要对时间安排做一些修改，我希望与您研究后再进行修改。
- 我们需要就这些更改做出决定。

有时可以省略邮件的正文部分，直接要求会面。

结尾

这一部分具体制定实施计划。要尽可能详细，并且可以提供一些额外的信息。例如，必要时可以提供你的办公电话或移动电话。

- 明早可以一起开会讨论吗？
- 我周一会去市中心，希望能与您会面。您可以给我发邮件或者打我的手机，号码是……。

- 本周何时方便会面？
- 3 月 14 日你和________有空参加会议吗？如果你想要讨论一些备选方案而我又没有时间的话，请联系我的助理________。他有我的日程表，并且可以安排一个对你来说方便的时间。

当然，有时你不得不通过电子邮件传达坏消息。此时邮件的标题和首句可以采用上述句式，但其他部分请使用以下完美措辞。

主体

为其界定谈话的范围，这样他们就知道将会面对什么。例如你可以说：

- 最近有三件事进展得不太顺利，我们必须处理一下。第一……
- 在随后的几周里，我们需要处理以下一些意外的变化……
- 由于……必须在你们的原计划上做五个小小的改动。
- 预算金额比我们最初预计的要高一些，原因在于以下两点……

然后告诉他们你打算如何处理这种情况：

- 下一步我们将给你们提供一份修订好的计划。
- 尽管有这些变化，我们仍将继续进行。
- 我们的团队将于周二开会，并且在周三以书面的形式将这些变化通知您。
- 我们将在周一与公司会计会面，确定一些最可行的应急对策来尽量减少费用。

结尾

不管未来情形如何，都要清楚地告诉收件人你将于何时再次与其联系，这可以使对方觉得你可以控制局势。

- 我们将在周一的会议之后与您联系，告诉您最新的消息。
- 我将在周四给您打电话，以确认您是否收到了邮件。
- 给您发送最新拟定的财务方案之后，我将打电话给您询问是否有问题。
- 我们一旦获得了进一步的消息会马上回复您，最晚在本月 10 日。

开会处理有争议的问题

无论你要传达的是什么样的消息，都要用友好的语气开场，让与会者感到自己受到重视。

- 我觉得让各位了解一下……很重要。
- 我们认为你们应该最先获知……
- 我们确信媒体很快就会注意到这一点，所以希望你们能直接从我们这里获知……
- 人们正在私下议论，我觉得应该让你们知道真相。

然后告诉他们相关的坏消息。

你的团队在某些方面失误了

如实相告。显而易见这要取决于实际情况，但总的来说措辞要直接且简短。

- 由于硬件故障，电脑上的数据丢失了，我们本应该进行备份的。
- 我们的分包商出错了，不得不重新打一遍地基。
- 我们公司总裁卷入了内幕交易，媒体很快就会发现这一点。
- 我们关于……的预言是错误的。

然后告诉对方你下一步的打算，可能的话强调该失误能给对方带来的好处。

- 我们将在随后的两周内重新录入这些信息，这将是一次重新核对数据的好机会，可以借此删除过时或无关的信息。
- 他已对解决措施进行了复核，并且采取了正确的……
- 我们准备集思广益，开展一场声势浩大的公关活动。本活动将会强调我们团队的道德观。
- 最终，我们将有更多的方式来预测走势。

根据听众的反应，不时询问一下他们是否有疑问。这可以使对方感到自己在掌控局势，并且会觉得你没有对他们隐瞒信息。

- 任何人有任何问题都可以提出来。
- 欢迎大家提问。

- 如果有问题的话请举手，我会叫你们的。
- 我非常乐于回答你们的问题，如果你们时间不够的话，也可以会后找我。
- 我愿意回答你们的所有问题，如果会后还有问题的话，可以给我发电子邮件。

小提示

不要说那些使局面恶化的词语，比如避免使用下列不必要的修饰语。

避免用语	参见例句
只	我们只完成了五个目标中的四个。
仅	您将仅能收到一半的报告。
不幸的是	不幸的是，我们没能预料到这一变化。

另外，不要加入主观评判，听众会有自己的想法。

避免用语	参见例句
可怕的	我们处理这一可怕局面的唯一办法是……
令人不快的	我们必须应对这一令人不快的事态变化。
不幸的	由于这种不幸的情况……
差劲的	这一差劲的结局表明……

顾客在公司接待室大声抱怨时，员工向你求助

这种情况会令所有人不安，包括你本人、你的员工、吵闹的人、接待室里的其他人以及随后听说此事的亲友们。所以，你必须马上平息事态。第一步，注意你的举止。的确，你的内心正在畏缩，但是外表只能保持镇静，处之泰然。更难的情况你都处理过，嘿！这不过是小菜一碟。的确有点棘手，但仍旧是小菜一碟。然后请使用以下完美措辞，通常可按本文顺序使用。

让客户冷静下来

- 请原谅，有什么可以帮您的吗？
- 对不起，我能和您谈谈吗？
- 我无意中听到您有些生气，我很愿意和您谈谈这一问题。

小提示

如果与配偶或孩子发生争吵，在对方怒火中烧时要求其冷静下来，只会适得其反，他/她会变得更加激动。所以，最好不要提这个建议，而是承诺你会把问题解决好。

- 我保证能解决这一问题。
- 我想知道是什么问题，并且看看我们能否解决。
- 如果您与这里的某位员工之间有什么问题的话，我觉得我们应该加以解决。
- 让我们看看能帮您做些什么。

要求该员工私下与你谈话

- 去我的办公室好吗？我们可以一起谈谈。
- 去那边的椅子坐会儿怎么样？我们谈谈。
- 去休息室坐一会儿好吗？一起喝杯咖啡。
- 如果你现在没时间的话，以后可以随时找我谈这事。

让该员工冷静下来

情况往往如此：你在平息顾客的同时，也不想让其他人看该员工的笑话。因此与该员工交谈时，一定要表达信任，态度随和而平静。通常一两句简单的话就行。可能的话，你可以直呼其名，这样可以显出你理解对方。

- 谢谢，________。
- 你还好吧，________？很好！
- 我们会解决好这件事的，________。继续工作吧。
- 我过后会和你谈谈的，________。

在会议上，与会者要求你解释公司发生的一桩丑闻

职场上发生了丑闻或与之相关的棘手事情时，这当然不是你的错。你并没有撒谎，是首席执行官撒了谎；你并没有桃色事件，是你的老板；你并没有欺骗股东，是董事长做的。但是偏偏就是你！你正忙于本职工作，忽然被问起这一丑闻。这可能发生在会议上，在产品推销活动中，或是在演讲过程中。你的确是公司代言人，对吧？那该怎么办呢？就像面对其他困境一样，运用以下完美措辞，表现镇定，积极发言。

感谢对方提出这一问题

政客们总是如此。但是不要让你的工作受到此细节影响。向对方致谢，这样会表明你态度坦率，与此事无关，愿意谈论此事。此外，你的确感谢他们的提问，对吧？毕竟这给了你一个机会，你能够以有利于自己的方式谈论大家关注的事情。

- 感谢您的提问，我很乐于讲述这一问题。
- 感谢您提到这一问题，我知道每个人都在想这件事。
- 您能提到这一点很好，我知道每个人都想了解这件事。
- 我本没想到要讲这个问题，所以很高兴您能提出来。
- 很高兴能有机会讨论一下事态的进展。
- 是的，新闻里刚刚报道了此事，你们都已经知道发生了什么事，对吧？（如果有人不知道的话，尽可能实事求是地解释一下。）

使自己置身事外

- 我和你们一样，只知道一点。
- 说实话我也感到很惊讶。
- 这一事态并没有影响到我所在的部门。
- 我的部门里没有人参与此事，所以我们知之甚少。
- 我只是听说了一些事情，我很愿意把这些告诉大家。（当然，都是无害的或者公开的。）

- 的确有很多猜测，但是你们所享受的服务不会有任何变化。
- 尽量像我这样做，决不相信谎言和猜测，只相信亲眼所见的。在我看来，一切都会化险为夷的。

告诉他们最好和最坏的可能，这样就可以引导他们的预期

最坏的

- 从现在起，你们肯定会在媒体上看到大量的报道。
- 短期内我们的股票会下跌，但是我向你们保证一定会反弹的。
- 毫无疑问，人们会议论纷纷，但是请不要相信这些议论。
- 人们对这些事总是会往坏处想。

最好的

- 我们团队适应力强，我相信一切都会过去的。
- 这可能意味着我们需要做出一些改变，但是请相信，一切都将向好的一面发展。
- 即使……真的发生了，我们也会挺过去的。以前也发生过这种事情，我们都坚持下来了。
- 通常情况下，这种事只会让我们更坚强。

错误做法：

- 猜测为什么会发生这种情况。
- 表示关切。
- 为此事道歉。
- 私下谈论此事。
- 抨击所知道的任何卷入此事的人。

正确做法：

- 表现出公正的态度。
- 对自己的公司保持尊重。

- 强调一下你是一名业务人员而不是新闻发言人。
- 不要做任何评价（不管是好的还是坏的）。

新闻界让你谈论你们行业所面临的某个问题

如果不是在公关部门的话，你不应该随便回答新闻界的问题，即使是当地大学的小报也不行。但是，偶尔你会发现自己正面临这种困境：某位记者向你提出关于市场方面的问题，或者是关于你们公司在业内地位的问题以及诸如此类的问题。如果不能礼貌地、巧妙地回避这些问题，你就必须得给予答复。以下这些完美措辞可以为你打开一扇方便之门，帮你干净利落地脱身。

当记者首次提及此问题

- 您应该与我们的公关部门讨论此事，可以在网上找到他们的联系电话。
- 作为一名……我对此并不了解内情，也无法做出评论。
- 如果您想知道那件事的话，可以登录我公司网站的问答页面，在那里会找到答案。
- 这些都是很好的问题，您可以去联系一下________。
- 如果您过后给我发个电子邮件的话，我可以提供给您一个合适的人选，他将为您的文章提供资料。

如果记者继续追问

保持冷静和友好的态度，这样可以显出你没什么要隐瞒的。

- 对不起，我已经说过了，你应该联系我们新闻部门的________。
- 有很多人问了大量的问题，但是正如我所说的，我无法回答这些问题。
- 我很乐于澄清这些事情，但是我此刻实在没什么可说的。
- 我很愿意回答你的问题，但现在我不能这样做。

若你同意与媒体会面

有时候你愿意接受采访，但是记者的问题可能会使你陷入困境，比如让你对老板发表一些负面评价。以下妙语有助于你摆脱困境。

- 我不能那么说。
- 那与本话题无关。
- 我对此问题无可奉告。你还有别的问题吗？
- 无可奉告，下一个问题。
- 没什么可说的。

你成为某一问题或其他棘手情况的关键人物，而你并不清楚怎么会这样

也许这一问题源于你们团队，也许是负责人外出了，由你临时替补。不管怎样，已然如此了，你成了一个毫不知情的关键人物。以下完美措辞有助于你表现得胸有成竹，并且可使你避免说出一些纯粹的臆测或老套的猜想。

当你需要把球踢给别人

要让对方明确地知道你在向其介绍最佳人选。一位高层人士，一位再合适不过的人。

- 我很想帮忙，但是________才是合适的人选。
- 最适合与您讨论此问题的是________。
- 您可以给________打个电话，并且告诉我相关进展。
- 我对此情况知之甚少，________知道得更多一些，您可以在本周联系他。

可能的话就直接联系。

- ________是我们在该领域的最高负责人，他能够帮助您。我会给他发个邮件，并且抄送给您，这样您就可以联系他了。

● 我会给________打个电话，告诉他我们已经谈过以及具体的谈话内容。这样，您在下周早些时候就可以与他取得联系了。

● 我会给________打电话，并且请他电话联系您，您什么时候方便？

● 我收到了您的关于“……”的邮件，并且将其转发给了________，他是我们在该领域的专家。他明天会联系您。

要尽可能详细，显然具体细节取决于你所谈论的内容，以下给出了一些示例。

● 我们财务部的________会与您联系，告诉您如何正确填写这些表格以及如何弥补相关损失。

● 我会让________告诉您需要采取的三个步骤，照此办理就可以重新走上正轨。

● ________供职于我们公司的法律事务部。他知道您应该采取的最佳应对方法，请等待他与您联系。在此之前不要向任何人发邮件或者谈论此事。如果他没有联系您，请通知我，我会联系他。

● 当您采取进一步措施之前，需要更多地了解自己所面临的选择。您可以给________发邮件，他会告知您相关事宜。

你需要了解更多的信息后再答复对方

不要让对方觉得你不清楚自己在做什么，不要让其看出你是在代人受过，或者你只是个小角色。这样会引起更大的不安，并且会有损于你以及其他人的职业生涯。

错误用语：

● 我确实一无所知。

● 他们怎么会让你找我？我根本就不在那个部门。

● 我怎么会知道！

● 说实话，我不知道，这超出了我的专业范畴。

● 嗯？（表示不懂）

● 谁让你们来找我的？为什么？

- 真希望我能帮你，但你没那么走运。

正确用语：

- 我在做出回应之前需要了解更多的信息。
- 让我先核实几件事情，然后再与您联系。
- 我在处理这一事件之前需要先澄清几点想法。
- 这很有意思。我回头再答复您，这样我会把全部的细节弄清楚。
- 我想就此事问一下我的同事，他是一位专家，可以提供最佳的信息。

一定要给出明确的日期、时间以及沟通渠道，否则对方会觉得自己受到怠慢，被人遗忘。

- 我会在 24 小时之内答复您。
- 一旦从他那获得信息，我会马上给您发邮件。
- 无论如何，我会在一周之内给您发邮件。
- 我周五一大早就把邮件抄送给________，并且会继续跟进。

尽可能使用第一人称“我们”而不是第二人称“你们”，这样可以显得你把帮助他们解决问题视为己任。

- 我会给________打电话，我们可以从他那获得确切信息。
- ________一定能帮上忙，他会很快与我们联系。
- 我想我们能在本周末解决这一问题。
- 我们会很顺利地得到您所需要的最新消息，我会把细节反馈给您。

当对方很恼火

无论你是多么乐于和解，一个人发火时一般很难领会你所说的话。如果此人是别人推给你的，情况就会更糟。很可能他已经与别人谈过了，他会越来越沮丧。

首先要让对方感到安心，然后再询问信息。

- 好的，您已经找对地方了，现在告诉我究竟发生了什么事。
- 好的，请不要担心，我一定会帮助您的，请您从头说起吧。

● 很高兴您能与我联系，我保证您能得到正确的答案。究竟发生了什么事？

● 感谢您与我联系，我们一定能把问题处理好，请告诉我发生了什么事。

● 让我们来解决它吧，告诉我是什么问题，不要遗漏任何细节。

如果你不明白该人所说的话，那就请对方澄清一下。要确保他能明白你这样做是为了帮助他们，而不是由于不了解情况或是漠不关心。

● 您能再提供一些细节吗？这样我就能弄清楚您所说的事了。

● 我想再问您几个问题，这样我就能够确切知道目前的状况。

● 我想要弄清楚您刚才所说的话。您能否再重复一下最后一点？

● 请把刚才的内容重复一遍，我来确认一下细节。

● 在您继续讲述之前，我有几个问题想问……

一定要准确地了解该人的最终目的。由于这超出了你的职业范畴，所以要不露声色地询问。

● 您真正需要的是什么？

● 我怎样做才能帮助您？

● 我采用什么样的方法能帮助您解决这一问题？

● 目前，什么样的事态是您所希望的？

● 听起来您是想达到以下三点……

需要和老板讨论朋友、同事或员工转来的问题

总的来说该人是个好员工，并且你不想损害对方的名誉。

这是一种两难的境地，要十分谨慎。你不想指责一个好员工是不负责任的或是不称职的，当然，你也不想使该人的奖金或者晋升机会受到影响。但那人又必须负责，该怎么办？以下是一些答案。

保持客观

你在陈述自己的观点时一定要尽量公正，这一点很重要。所以要依据事实，即完全从客观的角度看待所发生的事情。如何判断是否客观呢？本质上讲就是可以衡量或者是可以证明的。当你保持客观时，就能明白

存在的问题，清楚你或其他人可以采取的补救措施。不要进行评判，所以要避免使用那些评价性的用语，要直奔主题。

错误用语：

- ________确实做了一些蠢事。
- 昨天，________在接待室里对客户态度无礼。
- ________的失误蠢得出奇。
- ________确实失误了。
- 我简直无法相信所发生的事。

正确用语：

实际用语取决于你所处的环境，以下只是一些例句。

- ________删除了一些含有会计信息的文件。
- 昨天，________让客户闭嘴。
- ________忘记了锁保险柜。
- ________没有完成方案。
- 以下是我的个人观点……

指出预期后果

- ________需要尽快重新录入文件。
- ________需要参加顾客服务培训课程。
- 需要在保险柜上贴提醒标签。
- ________要负责完成后续的所有方案。
- ________需要保证类似的事不再发生。

提醒老板这种行为只是偶然现象，不要使用负面的词语描述当事人。

- ________平时办事很精明的。
- ________通常很善于与人打交道。
- ________其实很注意安全。

要以事实或可观察到的信息作为根据。

- 这种情况以前从未发生过。
- ________通常很有礼貌并且举止得体。
- 在此以前________从未在安全方面出过问题。

Part Three

In the Spotlight—(and Not Sure How You Got There)

These things happen. You're going about your day and suddenly get a call—a colleague just broke his leg—and you need to fill in for him or her at a conference. Or you're setting up for a talk and realize you left your slides back at the office—a six-hour plane ride away. There you are, in the spotlight, with nowhere to hide. Before you make a fool of yourself or otherwise disappoint or disgrace your company, remember these perfect points—then read the perfect phrases for bailing you out of any difficult situation, no matter how glaring the spotlight.

- **Take your time.** Sometimes the spotlight is immediate—like that situation where you're present but the slides are not. Rather than dive ahead, give yourself a moment to strategize about how you'll manage the situation. Admit that you forgot them? Pretend that somehow the airline lost them? Or move into the discussion as if you never intended to use them in the first place?

- **Remain composed.** Regardless of the situation, don't give away your discomfort by fidgeting, sighing loudly, or scratching your face, head, or throat. Instead, stand straight and smile as you make eye contact with one of the participants. But—if you must—engage in a meaningful activity to burn off the energy, such as organizing your paper or preparing a fresh page on the flip chart.

- **Don't overapologize.** The worst thing you can do is draw unwarranted attention to your faux pas. So if the situation does call for an "I'm sorry," say it quickly and move on. Remember, everyone makes mistakes or doesn't have all the information necessary when others need it. So do the best you can with confidence and control. And remember, don't fidget (see the second bullet point above).

● **Refer them to another authority when appropriate.** Say, someone asks a question and you have no idea about the answer. This is your subject, after all. You should know the answer, right? Give the best answer you can under the circumstance, and refer the person to someone else. Or even better, track down the answer, and e-mail or call later. It will show you're professional and caring. If the press calls about a sticky situation, better have someone from the press room—who can give the right answers in the right way—call back.

● **Follow up. Always follow up.** Forget your slides? Run out of handouts? Have a question from the press you couldn't answer so you sent the reporter to someone else? Doesn't matter—always follow up. Call the press person in your company to make sure he or she connected with your colleague—even if the questions are hostile. This will prove that you're cooperative and have nothing to hide. Forget handouts or slides? Then get the names and addresses of participants at the seminar, and send them a copy. Depending on why you're giving the presentation, this could also prove to be a great business opportunity: send them a note or business card, and tweak their interest in calling you for help.

You're in Front of a Group and Feel Utterly Incompetent—and Unprepared

This happens from time to time—even though you really are a consummate professional, an expert in your field, and a real stand-up performer. Still, you walk in the room thinking you're going to address a group of new (and inexperienced) employees and find yourself facing a group of older and wiser senior VPs. Or you got talked into giving a presentation because you were the most knowledgeable . . . because you knew a little and everyone else in your company knew nothing at all. So there you are, standing at a whiteboard, podium, or Web camera with who knows how many quizzical gazes focusing in on you. What do you do?

When the heat is on, stay cool within by closing your mouth and telling yourself these perfect phrases:

● I can do this—I've done harder things with great success before.

● I know the content inside and out—whatever I say can be helpful.

● I have to trust myself to do the best I can—that's about all I can do.

- This will be a great experience either way.
- People usually like my talks—so the odds are, they'll like this one, too.
- What three things can I do to manage this situation? (Then give yourself an answer, perhaps starting with "drink some water" or "open by asking them to say what they want from the session.")

Remember

Don't fidget or fuss. Stand tall, strong, and confident.

Scope Out Your Territory

It's important that you have control over the session. So determine what aspect of the talk you want to focus on—or omit. If that's the case, and you have a PowerPoint presentation, you may have to toss one or two of the slides or briefly touch on the points and then keep going. Just make sure you feel comfortable with the direction or territory of your talk.

When introducing the content, be sure to tell your audience what you'll discuss and how they'll benefit from hearing about it:

- You'll be able to apply new models to your business growth with the seven principles we'll review today.
- In today's session, we're going to review _____ so you can _____.
- With the ____ that's we'll cover today, you will get three results.
- The information which I'll review today has helped departments like yours reach these success points.
- With the strategies I'll present today, you will be able to achieve_____.
- The information you'll hear in this session is new and unexplored in any way by your competitors.

Be specific to add credibility to your message and better manage your listeners' expectations:

Don't

- You will learn things that will help your organization do better.

●In this seminar, I will cover subject matter that will bring results.

Do

●You will learn seven strategies for accelerating your profitability in the current downturn.

●In this seminar, I will cover strategies from three influential leaders that you can use to grow your business by up to 125 percent within a year.

Establish the Rules

Are you comfortable with people interrupting you with questions? Or would you prefer to answer them all at the end? The organization where you're speaking may have its own preference, but don't worry—you need to establish the rules. This will set you up as an authority and help you take control.

●Please save your questions to the end of the sessions.

●If you have any questions, please wait—I ask to hear them when it makes sense to break.

●I'll take questions just before the break.

●Feel free to ask questions as we go.

●If you have questions, raise your hand, and I'll call on you when we have finished the point.

When You Don't Know the Answer to a Question Either Because It's Not Relevant or You Simply Don't Know

●I'll get back to you about that question later.

●That question is outside of my expertise. I can find the answer and get back to you.

●That's a great question, but I want to address it later. (Find the answer at your break.)

●That's a great question, but it doesn't directly address the subject we're covering. Since we don't have much time, I can't address it now. Sorry.

●That question deserves a thorough answer—I'm not quite prepared to address it at this time.

You Don't Have the Required Slides, Handouts, or Other Copy for Your Presentation

People expect goodies when they attend a presentation: a book, handouts, worksheets, tip sheets, and so on. Who knows? Maybe they dump them in the waster later, or maybe they fastidiously take notes in the margin and save them straight through to retirement. Either way, they expect them. And if you don't produce, they feel cheated. Even worse, the distaste will last throughout the session, tingeing their experience no matter how well you do. So here are some steps—with perfect phrases—to make up for the lack—and then some.

Apologize

You have to say something, right? So a quick apology will demonstrate your sincerity. Don't overdo it. Be short and sweet with perfect phrases like these:

- My apologies—I don't have the handouts with me today.
- I'm going to give the talk without slides today. My apologies.
- Sorry—I don't have the handouts with me . . .
- We're going to look at some examples—I'll write them on the whiteboard since I'm sorry to say I don't have the worksheets here today.
- I'm sorry—I didn't pack the support material as I was preparing for this talk.

Avoid Putting Too Glaring a Spotlight on the Mistake, by Not Saying Things Like

Don't say . . .	As in . . .
I forgot	Darn, I forgot to bring the worksheets.
I can't believe . . .	I can't believe I did (or didn't) do this.
Boy am I . . .	Boy am I spacey . . . Boy am I frazzled . . . Boy am I stupid today.

Don't say ...	As in ...
It must be because ...	It must be because I'm really wiped out. It must be because I'm so busy. It must be because my assistant's out and I can't keep up with details.
I do this ...	I never do this. I always do this. I do this every time I'm traveling a lot.

Explain When Appropriate

If the reason is good, interesting, and not about your emotional or personal state—go ahead. Otherwise, skip this step. The perfect phases will depend on your situation. Here are some examples that can help:

● My suitcase with the handouts never arrived at the airport. Hopefully, I'll get it soon.

● My office was shut down the day before I was leaving, and I couldn't get in to get the notes.

● Someone stole my briefcase at the airport. (The oldest excuse in the book—but say it if it's true.)

Promise a Replacement Later—or Even Something Better!

To soothe the pain, however minimal that pain may be, say that you'll send the handouts or the PowerPoint slides. Don't offer—promise, plain and simple. That way you'll have control over the situation and can ensure they won't say no.

Don't Offer

● If you like, I can send you the handouts next week.

● Would you like me to get you those PowerPoints anyway?

● Just give me your e-mail address after the session if you want copies.

● If you still want copies, leave me your e-mail or mailing address, and I'll send them along.

Promise

● I'll get you the handouts first thing next week.

● I'll get you those PowerPoints right away.

● Give me your e-mail address after the session so I can get you the copies.

● Leave me your e-mail or mailing address, and I'll send the copies right away.

If Possible, Explain to Your Audience the Value of Getting the Handouts Late

● You will get the worksheets on Friday. Why not try a few examples: you can test how much you remember and have an easier time applying the information to your work.

● I'll e-mail the PowerPoint presentation so you can add it to your notes.

● I'll send the case studies right away so you can compare them to your situations at work.

Either Way, Avoid Using Negating Terms That Downplay Your Future Actions

Negating terms	As in . . .
The least	The least I can do is e-mail you the worksheets.
Unfortunately . . .	Unfortunately, I'll have to e-mail the case studies later.
Sorry to say . . .	Sorry to say, I can only send them when I return next week.
I cannot . . . until . . .	I cannot get them to you until next week.

When possible—and try to make it possible!—send a little extra. This shouldn't cost you extra, and you'll cash in on lots of goodwill!

Tell your audience what you're sending and how it helps:

● I'm also sending along a series of case studies that will help you apply the content to additional situations.

● I am sending you a copy of a book I wrote so you can see how PR actually helps enhance your customer service.

● In addition, you'll receive a PowerPoint presentation that provides background to today's talk.

You don't have to be direct, by the way. Just be impressive. The content will depend on what you send, of course. Here are a few examples:

● You'll also get a copy of our company president's speech to the Committee on Safety which won accolades from the ***New York*** Times business section.

● I'm sending you a tape called "Set Yourself Straight: 10 Strategies for Self-Motivation." Over 40,000 people have used the information here to improve their lives and make their fortunes!

Follow Up

You should follow up for lots of reasons. One is to ensure that your audience received your material. Who knows, maybe it got accidentally swallowed up by their spam filter or destroyed by an overly zealous "delete" key. So better check. Also, you want them to remember you—and think highly of you when they do. This could lead to yet another advantage: they may hire you, as a result. But be discreet—you want your follow up to be a sincere inquiry—not a sales pitch.

When Calling

Remind them of who you are:

● I gave the talk _______ at the ______ last week.

● I am the sales rep for ______.

● I was the speaker at the seminar ______.

Tell them what you sent.

● I wanted to make sure you received the slides that I promised plus one of our gold-plated pens.

● Just want to be sure that you received the e-mailed worksheets that I sent on Thursday.

● Please let me know if you received our package on ______ last Tuesday.

When E-Mailing

They know who you are from the letterhead on your e-mail or your e-mail address. So remind them of your talk, and ask whether they received the content.

- Hope you enjoyed the conference in Atlanta and that you received the handouts from my seminar ______.
- Hope you have been well since the seminar last week. Did you get the worksheets that I sent on Wednesday?
- Just to let you know—I sent the case studies from my session ______ on Friday. Please let me know if you received them.

You Need to Prolong a Meeting—or Reconvene One via E-Mail—on a Difficult Topic

This happens more than you'd think. People start fidgeting, your time is up, but you need to keep going. In situations like these, you can't insist that people stay, but you can convince them. Other times, you may need to end the meeting earlier than optimal and must send an e-mail bringing the gang back together. Either way, here are some perfect phrases for taking the edge off a clock that keeps tick-tick-ticking.

When You Know You're About to Go Over

Give them a time frame so they know what to expect, and explain why they should stay. When possible, stress the positive aspect of the situation—especially if controversy, hurt feelings, and even anger may be hovering in the air. Show what you plan to accomplish and why it will ultimately help everyone along.

- We only have 10 more minutes, and I still have two more points I don't want you to miss. So let's go until quarter past the hour; then we'll break.
- Don't start putting your notebooks away yet; we need to go for an extra 10 minutes. Then everyone will know who is responsible for what, and the project should flow smoothly.
- Let's plan to end this session 5 minutes late so I can address all your questions.
- Why don't we keep going until 9:30 so we can address those important issues that ____ and ___ just raised.

I think we will all benefit from reviewing them.

● We really need to settle these budget issues before we leave so the project can finally be launched. So let's plan to go until 12:00.

● So we can wrap up with a solid game plan, let's plan to stay for an extra 20 minutes or so.

Quick tip

Give wiggle room to those who need really need to head out, but make sure they get any information they missed:

● If you have a client meeting, I understand that you'll need to go. Just be sure to get notes from one of your colleagues.

● Those of you who take the 3:00 shuttle, go ahead and leave on time. Who can get them the notes?

● If you have a high-priority meeting, go ahead, but find someone who will give you meeting notes.

● If you must leave, be sure to get a list of our goals for next week; you'll be responsible either way.

● We'll be giving out assignments at the end of the meeting; if you need to go, I understand, but we'll assign you a responsibility.

You're Over the Time Limit and Want to Keep Them from Leaving

Think limit, purpose.

Limit **Purpose**

● Could you guys wait 10 more minutes? We have an important decision to make.

● We only need about 10 more minutes, and your input on the proposal will be critical.

● Hold on everyone—we need ten more minutes or so to come to a conclusion before everyone leaves.

● We can't stop yet—we need at least 15 more minutes, or we'll lose our momentum.

You Need to Finish the Session Another Time

Be definite about when you're meeting next—or how you intend to reach people to decide.

Don't

- We didn't complete everything—we'll need to meet again.
- Someone will be back in touch with you to figure out a good time to finish this up.
- Let's get together and finish this discussion sometime soon.

Do

- We need more time to cover everything—please mark your calendars for the same time and place next week.
- We need to complete our goals list. _______, will you get back to everyone tomorrow about the time that works best?
- We have to complete this budget by Monday. Send me a time that works best for you on Friday morning, and I'll figure something out.
- Let _______know tomorrow whether you can meet next Thursday. If not, we'll meet on Friday, but no later.
- We need to reconvene on Thursday at 2:00. If you can't make it, let me know. But because of time issues, you'll lose your vote.

You Need to Reconvene the Meeting through an E-Mail

Remind them of the last meeting, what you need to complete your agenda, and when you're holding it:

- Since we ran out of time at the May 14 meeting, we still need to determine the budget for our project. So we will meet again on May 21 at 3:00 in the ______ Conference Room.
- Our goal for the all-hands meeting was to determine an implementation strategy for_______. While we came up with some great ideas, we still need to develop a concrete strategy. Let _______know when you are available next week.
- At the May 19 meeting, we decided to contact _______ with a finished

proposal. So that we can stick to our plan, we will need to meet on Tuesday.

● As you know, we ran over time at Tuesday's meeting. So that we can determine next steps and keep the program on track, we must meet again this Tuesday.

Quick tip

Use positive language, focusing on what can happen, rather than what didn't happen. This can project a feeling of optimism—especially important when people are feeling disgruntled or otherwise grim. Notice the subtle but important difference:

Don't

● We didn't finish allocating the budget.

● We never clarified the correct procedure in those situations.

● Mary didn't get an answer to her last question.

Do

● We need to finish allocating the budget.

● We must clarify the correct procedure in those situations.

● Mary should get an answer to her last question.

Your Colleagues Ask You to Address a Situation That You Know the Audience Won't Like

Well, someone's got to do it, as the old saying goes. And why shouldn't it be you? Okay, you can think up a dozen reasons why it shouldn't be you: maybe you're not qualified, maybe the situation is just too complicated, or maybe you simply don't like controversy. You have enough headaches, right? But there you are on the hot seat—and face it, everyone gets there some time. These perfect phrases should help cool you down—and will help you with addressing other tense situations, too.

When Addressing the Controversial Issue in an E-Mail

It's always best to address a difficult situation in person; you can look at the audience's response, see their reactions, and manage your comments according to how they feel. If they look alarmed, for example, you can put them at ease with a comment, a smile, or a sympathetic look. Not so with writing. They may be shrieking with rage or nodding with sad understanding—how would you know, though? So your best option would be to ask them for a time when you can discuss the situation face-to-face. Here are some perfect phrases that can help.

Subject Line

Keep the subject line fast and informative; you want them to pay attention and open your e-mail, but you don't want them to be alarmed. Use strong verbs and a forward-looking approach when possible—or just ask for a meeting:

- Project X changes
- Can we meet on Monday?
- New information on ___
- New directions for ___
- Plan changes—can we discuss?
- Meeting about developments—Thursday?

First Line

This line will set a tone for the rest of your e-mail. Try not to be too gloomy or alarmist—remember, you need to keep your audience's confidence so that they'll respond in the calmest, most effective way:

- We have just learned of changes to the project ____ that we need to discuss.
- I was hoping to meet you early next week to discuss some recent matters regarding our budget.
- We have just gathered some important information about our project for ___.
- We need to adapt our timeline for the ____.
- ____ called earlier today; he has some important information that I would like to discuss with you.

Body of the Message

Add any details that might be helpful—but not too many. Remember, your mission is to get them to meet with you ASAP so you can spill the beans in the most productive way—not to dump information they won't like. Make sure the recipients know their role in the discussion:

- The ______ has changed their mind about several aspects of the project, and we need to discuss what our next steps should be.
- The funding has shifted on several fronts, which I can tell you about in detail.
- We need to make several changes to our timeline. I would like to review these with you before taking any steps.
- We need to make some decisions regarding these changes.

Sometimes, you may need to forget the body of the e-mail altogether and just ask for the meeting.

Closing

This is where you make the concrete plans. Be as specific as possible, and provide additional information, such as your office or cell phone, when necessary.

- Can you meet tomorrow morning to discuss?
- I will be in town on Monday and would like to see you then. You can e-mail me or reach me on my cell at______.
- When is the best time for us to meet this week?
- Would you and _____ be available to meet on March 14? If you want to discuss some options and I'm not available, please contact my assistant, ______. He has my schedule and will find a time that works best for you.

Sometimes, of course, you have to deliver the bad news electronically. Keep your subject and first lines more or less the same as when you're requesting a meeting, but change the rest using perfect phrases like these.

Body of the Message

Give them boundaries for the discussion so they know what's ahead. So, for example, you might say:

- We have three issues that cropped up recently that we must address. First . . .
- Within the next few weeks, we are going to address these unexpected changes . . .
- Because of ______, we need to make five small changes to your original plan.

● The budget will be higher than we originally predicted for these two reasons:

Then let them know how you plan to address the situation:

● Our next step is to give you a revised plan.

● We will continue moving ahead in spite of these changes.

● Our team will meet on Tuesday and have the changes to you, in writing, on Wednesday.

● We will meet with our accountants on Monday to determine the most expedient ways to minimize the expenses.

Closing

Regardless of the future, make sure your recipients are clear about when they will hear from you again. This will give them the sense you're in control.

● We will contact you after the meeting on Monday to fill you in.

● I will call you on Thursday to ensure you got the package.

● After I send you the new financial plan, I'll call to see if you have questions.

● We will be back with you about these changes the minute we know more—the 10th at the latest.

When Addressing the Controversial Issue in a Meeting

Start out warmly—letting the participants feel somehow special (in spite of the message you're about to deliver):

● I think it's important that you know . . .

● We thought you should be the first ones to hear about . . .

● We're pretty sure the media will get hold of this soon, and we wanted you to know directly from us . . .

● I know that people are gossiping a lot and thought you should know the facts.

Then tell them the bad news.

When Your Group Dropped the Ball Somehow

Tell them what happened—obviously this depends on your situation, but the phrases should be direct and quick:

● We needed to back up the information on our computer, and when the hard drive died, we lost the information.

● Our subcontractor made an error and will have to lay the foundation again.

● Our company president was involved in insider trading, and the media's about to find out.

● Our predictions were off by _____.

Then tell them what you plan to do next. Where possible, highlight any advantages they get from the mishap:

● We will reenter the information over the next two weeks. This will give us an opportunity to fact-check again and take out antiquated or irrelevant information.

● He will double-check the measurements and use the right _______.

● We're going to put together a really strong PR campaign that will underscore the ethical nature of our group, otherwise.

● Ultimately, we will have more access to the trends.

Depending on the response, periodically ask if they have questions. This will give them a sense of control and the feeling that you're not withholding information from them:

● If anyone has any questions, please ask.

● I welcome all your questions.

● If you have questions, please raise your hand and I'll call on you.

● I'm eager to take your questions. If you don't have enough time, please contact me after the meeting.

● I'd like to answer all your questions—if you have any after the meeting ends, please e-mail me.

Quick tip

Try to avoid language that aggravates the situation. For example, don't use unnecessary modifiers in cases like these:

Avoid	As in
Only	We only reached four of our five goals.
Just	You will receive just half of the report.
Unfortunately	Unfortunately, we didn't expect that shift.

Also, try not to add value judgments; your audience will make their own assertions.

Avoid	As in
Terrible	The only way we can address this terrible situation . . .
Miserable	We must address this miserable turn of events . . .
Unfortunate	Because of this unfortunate situation . . .
Pathetic	The pathetic results prove that . . .

An Employee Turns to You for Help When a Customer Starts Complaining—Loudly—in the Lobby of Your Business

This situation is unsettling for everyone—you, your employee, the person who is carrying on, everyone else in the lobby, and those friends and family members who get to hear all about it later. So it's up to you to diffuse the difficult situation immediately. First step: your demeanor. True, you're cringing inside, but let your face reveal nothing but calm control. You've addressed worse—hey, this is a piece of cake. Okay, a bitter piece of cake, but still. Then use these perfect phrases—usually in the order that you'll find them here.

Calm the Customer

● Excuse me, is there a problem that I can help you with?

● Pardon me, do you think we could talk?

● I couldn't help overhearing that you were upset. I'd like to talk with you about it.

Remember

If you've ever been in an argument with a spouse or child, telling an upset person to calm down can have the opposite effect—he or she will get even more excited. So best to avoid that suggestion, and instead assure the customer that you can work out the problem:

● I'm sure we can figure this out.

● I'd like to know the problem to see if we can solve it.

● If you're having problems with one of the employees here, I think we should address the issue.

- Let's figure out what we can do to help.

Request That the Employee Speak to You Privately

- Why don't you come in my office, and we'll discuss this together?
- How about sitting on the chair over there, and we'll talk.
- Why not sit in the break room, and we'll have a cup of coffee?
- If you don't have time to talk now, feel free to contact me if you want to talk later.

Calm the Employee

Often, you need to disengage the customer without making the employee look foolish in the eyes of everyone else. So be sure to address the employee with trust, familiarity, and calm. Frequently, a simple word or two will do—call the employee by his or her name when possible to show that you connect.

- Thanks, _______.
- You okay, _____? Great.
- We'll figure this out, _____. Go ahead back to work.
- I'll talk to you later, _______.

At a Meeting, Participants Ask You to Explain a Scandal That Occurred at Your Company

When a scandal or related difficult situation occurs at work, you know it's not your fault. You didn't lie; your CEO did. You didn't have the affair; your boss did. And you didn't deceive the shareholders; that was the company president. Yet you, who were busy doing your job, suddenly get asked about the scandal at a meeting, during a sales pitch, or in the middle of a presentation. You do represent the company, right? So now what? Like anything else, be sure to project composure and willingness to talk by using these perfect phrases.

Thank Them for Asking or Bringing the Issue Up

Politicians do this all the time—but don't let that detail stop you. Thanking them will underscore your openness, lack of concern about the event, and willingness to talk. Besides, you really do appreciate their asking, right? After all, it gives you a chance to address what's on everyone's mind in a way that works to your advantage.

● Thanks for bringing this up. I'd like to address this situation.

● I appreciate your raising this issue—I'm sure everyone's thinking about it.

● Good thing you brought this up—I'm sure just about everyone wanted to.

● I wasn't about to raise the issue so I'm glad you brought it up.

● I appreciate the chance to discuss what's going on.

● Yes, this just came out in the news—do all of you know what happened? (If not, explain in the most factual way possible.)

Distance Yourself from the Situation

● I know about as little as you do.

● I was surprised, too, to tell you the truth.

● This situation doesn't affect anyone in my department.

● Since no one in my department was involved, we know very little about it.

● I only heard a few things, which I'll be happy to share with you. (Obviously, these are not damaging or confidential.)

● There's been quite a lot of speculation, but the service you receive will remain unchanged.

● Try to do what I do—don't trust rumor or speculation. Just see what's immediately in front of you. In my case, the coast will be clear.

Tell Them What They Can Expect—the Best and the Worst—to Manage Their Expectations

Worst

● I'm sure you'll hear lots on the media from now on.

● Our stocks may go down in the short run, but they'll bounce back, I can assure you.

● No question, people will be talking. But don't always trust what you hear.

- People always read the worst into these things . . .

Best

- We're a resilient group, and I'm sure this will blow over.
- This may mean we'll need to make changes—but trust me, they'll be for the better.
- Even if the _____ should happen, we'll survive. This has happened before, and look where we are now.
- Normally, events like these just make us stronger.

Do Not

- Speculate about why the situation happened.
- Express concern.
- Apologize for the event.
- Speak confidentially about the situation.
- Speak disparagingly about anyone you know who was involved.

Do

- Create an unbiased impression.
- Remain respectful of your company.
- Accentuate your role as a professional—not a spokesperson.
- Avoid making any judgments—good or bad.

A Newspaper Asks You to Discuss a Problem Confronting Your Industry

Unless you're in PR, you shouldn't be addressing questions from newspapers, even from your local college rag. But now and then, you'll find yourself in a difficult situation where a reporter asks about the market, your company's stand on an industry issue, or another matter. So, yes, you need to address the situation, if only to (politely and strategically) walk away. These perfect phrases will open the door for a clean exit.

When the Journalist First Asks the Question

● You need to talk to our PR Department. If you go online, you'll find the number.

● As a ____, I'm not privy to that kind of information, nor can I comment on it.

● If you want to know about that situation, go to the Q&A on our Web site. It has answers.

● Those are all very good questions. Why not contact ____?

● If you e-mail me later, I'll get you the right name of a source for your article.

If the Journalist Persists

Stay friendly and calm, so you don't look like you have something to hide:

● I'm sorry, but you'll need to contact ____ at our press room, as I mentioned.

● Lots of people are asking lots of questions. But as I said, I don't have any answers to give.

● I'd love to clarify these issues, but I simply don't have much to offer at this point.

● I'd love to answer your questions, but right now, I am not able to do so.

When You've Agreed to Meet with the Media

Sometimes you are willing to accept an interview. But the questions might put you in a difficult bind, like when you're asked to speak poorly about your boss. Here are some perfect comebacks that should get you off the hook:

● I can't speak to that.

● That isn't relevant to the discussion.

● I'll pass on that question. What else would you like to ask?

● No comment. Next question.

● I have nothing to say to that.

You're the Point Person for a Problem or Other Difficult Situation—but You're Not Sure Why

Maybe the problem originated with your group. Maybe the person in charge is out, so you're filling in. Either way, there you are, the point person with no answers to give. Here are some perfect phrases so you project a sense of control and can avoid dispensing information that's really conjecture or an old-fashioned guess.

When You Need to Pass the Buck

Be clear that you're sending them to the best possible person: one who's so high up the ladder, there's no place better for them to go.

- I'd like to help, but _____ is really a better person.
- The best person for you to talk about this is _____.
- Why don't you give _____ a call and get back to me about what happens.
- I know a little about the situation, but _____ knows more. Why not contact her this week?

When possible, directly make the connection:

- _____ is our senior most person in that area. He will be able to help you. I'll e-mail her and cc you to make the connection.
- I'll call _____ to let him know that we talked and fill him in on our discussion. Then you can get in touch with him early next week.
- I'll give _____ a call and have her call you. What time works best?
- I received your e-mail about ______ and forwarded it to ______. He is our expert in that area and will get in touch with you tomorrow.

Be specific whenever possible. Obviously, the particulars will depend on the content you're discussing, but here are some ideas:

- _____ in our Accounting Department will get back to you about the correct way you should have filled out that form and will tell you what you can do to repair the damage.
- I'll have _____ send you the three steps you need to take to get back on track.
- ______ is in our Legal Department and knows the best way for you to respond. Please wait for her to contact you before e-mailing or talking to anyone about the matter. If you don't hear from her, notify me and I'll be in touch.
- You'll need to learn more about your options before you progress. E-mail _____, who will send them to you.

When You Need to Get More Information and Get Back to Them

Be sure not to suggest that you don't know what you're doing, that someone made a mistake in passing your name along, or that you're junior level. This will only create more anxiety and make your life harder—and everyone else's, too.

Don't

- I really have no idea.
- Why would they send you to me? I'm not even in the right department.
- How on earth would I know?
- Honestly, I don't know. This just isn't my area of expertise.
- Huh?
- Who sent you to me—and why?
- Wish I could help you, but you're out of luck.

Do

- I'd like to get more information before I give a response.
- Let me check on a few things, and I'll be back in touch.
- I have a few points I need to clarify before I address this situation.
- This is interesting—let me get back to you so I get all the details straight.
- I'd like to ask my colleague about this; he is an expert and will be able to provide the best information.

Always give them a precise day, time, and communications vehicle—otherwise, they'll feel like you shoved them to the backburner where they'll languish, forgotten.

- I'll get back to you within 24 hours.
- Once I hear from her, I'll e-mail you.
- I'll e-mail you one way or the other within a week.
- I'll cc ___ on the e-mail and follow-up first thing on Friday.

Whenever possible, use the first person plural "we" instead of the second person "you." This shows that you feel personally involved in helping them solve the problem:

- I'll call ______. We should get precisely the right information from him.

- ______ is really helpful. She'll get back to us quickly.
- I think we should be able to solve this problem by the end of the week.
- We shouldn't have trouble getting the updates you need—let me get back to you with specifics.

When the Person Contacting You Is Upset

A person who's upset usually can't grasp what you're saying no matter how conciliatory you're trying to be. If someone sent that person to you, the plot only thickens; chances are the person's been talking to other people and the frustration has been mounting and mounting.

Reassure the person, and then ask for the information:

- Well, you came to the right place. Why don't you tell me what happened?
- Okay, well don't you worry; I'm going to help you. Why don't you start at the beginning?
- I'm so glad that you contacted me. I'll make sure you get the right answers. What exactly is going on?
- Thank you for contacting me. I know we can figure this out—so why don't you tell me what happened.
- Let's figure this out. Tell me the problem—don't leave out any details.

If you don't understand what the person is saying, ask for clarification. Make sure he or she knows you're asking so you can be helpful—not because you aren't informed or concerned.

- Can you give me details so I'm clear about what you're saying?
- Let me ask you a few questions so I know precisely what is going on.
- I want to be clear about what you just said—can you repeat that last point?
- Please repeat what you just said so I'm sure of the details.
- I have a few questions I want to ask before you continue . . .

Make sure you know precisely what the person wants as an outcome—since you're outside your area of expertise, this may not be apparent.

- What exactly do you need?
- How can I help you?
- In what ways can I help resolve the situation for you?

- What would you like to have happen now?
- It sounds like you need the following three things to happen . . .

You Need to Discuss a Problem with a Boss When a Friend, Colleague, or Employee Dropped the Ball

This person is usually a great worker, and you don't want to ruin his or her credibility.

You're in a bind that requires absolute discretion. You don't want to accuse a good worker of being irresponsible or of being a bad worker. Most certainly you don't want the person's bonus or promotion potential to be affected, either. Yet that person must be accountable. So what do you do? Here are some answers.

Be Objective

It's important that you state your point as fairly as possible. So rely on facts—what happened from a purely objective perspective. How do you know if it's objective? Essentially, you can measure or otherwise prove it. When you're objective, you give a clear idea of what went wrong and what you (or someone) can do to correct the situation—with no judgment involved. So avoid terms that reflect a value, and get straight to the point.

Do Not

- _____ did something really stupid . . .
- Yesterday, _____ was rude to a customer in the lobby.
- _____ made a ridiculously empty-headed mistake.
- _____ really dropped the ball.
- I couldn't believe what happened.

Do

The actual phrases will depend on your circumstances—here are some examples:

- _____ deleted the files with the account in it.
- Yesterday, _____ told a customer to shut up.

- _____forgot to lock the safe.
- _____ didn't complete the proposal.
- The following is what happened from my vantage point . . .

Show Desired Outcome

- _____ needs to reload the files as quickly as possible.
- _____ needs to go to a customer service training course.
- We need to put up reminders on the safe.
- _____ needs to be responsible for completing all proposals in the future.
- ______ needs to ensure that type of situation doesn't occur again.

Remind the Boss That This Behavior Was Unusual, but Do Not Use Negative Terms That Describe the Person

- _____ is usually so smart about things.
- _____ normally has a great way with people.
- _____ is really security-minded.

Do rely on factual or observable information:

- A situation like this never happened before.
- _____ is usually polite and appropriate.
- _____ has never had a security breech before this.

第四章

职场中遭遇个人不幸

职场中，人与人之间保持工作关系，没有私人交往。当然，我们也会谈论自己的孩子、抱负和度假经历，不过不会涉及过多细节。这些话题都不适合职场，也不是保持工作关系的关键。但是有时你不得不在工作中触及私事，尤其是同事遭遇厄运时。

沟通此类事情的难度超出多数人的想象。你必须既考虑情感因素，又要协调安排。你要放慢节奏，考虑到他人的感受或现实生活，你还要保证赶上期限，维持工作节奏。你的言辞要富有同情心，避免太煽情或不得体。的确，很难面面俱到。你该如何应对困境？请先阅读以下提示，然后我们再研究不同困境及化解它们的完美措辞。

● **要陈述，不要描述。**要客观表述所发生的事件，不要解释情况有多么糟糕，有多令人不快，有多么复杂。这就是陈述和描述的基本差异。描述事情时，你是从自己的观点解释情况，期望得到他人认可；而陈述事情时，你是要他人自己判断形势，得出正确的结论。

请注意其中的差异，读完本章完美措辞，你对此将会深有体会。

陈述：他的背部要做手术，还要接受几个星期的牵引治疗。

描述：他不得不接受痛苦的背部手术，这会令他精疲力竭。

● **具体交待后续安排。**如果同事生病，告诉对方会有人代为完工。联系其他人时，告诉对方该同事休假的时间以及具体帮工安排。

错误用语：在________休假期间，我们必须完成他所有的工作任务。

正确用语：明后两天我们必须用电子邮件把账单发出去，还要核查延误款项。

● **只对表面内容评论。**必须尊重同事的隐私权，让其自由决定是否表达自己的感受。这一点是至关重要的。当然表示同情总是很好的，只是方式要得体。

错误用语：我相信那样的确不舒服，尤其是你去洗手间时。

正确用语：听说了你遭受的痛苦，我也很难过。

同事被诊断出严重病情

这种情况可能是最为敏感的情况之一。同事得知不幸消息，面临痛苦，可能必须休假。你既不想唐突，也不想漠不关心。可以采用以下方法。

表达关心

可能你的同事很紧张，很想保护个人隐私，运用以下完美措辞化解困境，然后让你同事决定是说还是不说，只要对方感到舒服就好。

他人告知相关病情

● ________告诉了我你的病情，希望你不要太难过。

● 我刚听说你身体不太好，想问问情况。

● 你还好吗？我刚听说你患了________病。

● 我不想唐突或让你难堪，只是听说你身体不太好，想表示一下我的关心。

同事本人告诉你病情

● 听到这个消息我很难过。

● 难以置信！谢谢你告诉我。

● 真糟糕。你还好吗？

● 听到这种诊断结果，实在让人难过。

适当时表示鼓励

- 你看上去很健康，我相信你能战胜病魔。
- 你一直注意养生之道，想必你一定能战胜病魔。
- 你很明智，一定能寻求帮助最终战胜病魔。
- 我听说医生在治疗此类疾病上取得了重大进展。
- 目前已经有各种有益的治疗方案。

小提示

如果你知道有患者治愈过此类疾病，可以告诉该同事。得知他人克服了同样的困难，对其会有所帮助。

提供支持

通常情况下，轻松随意地提供帮助有助于让人感到关心，而不会干扰到他们的正常工作。

- 我如何帮你？
- 能为你做点什么？
- 你需要什么？
- 我如何帮你？

但是以上言辞也会让人感到缺乏诚意。因此，如果可能的话，尽量具体点。

- 你现在无法开车。要是去上班，我可以送你。
- 要是需要我上午为你代班，请告诉我。
- 要是你无法完成报告，我可以帮忙。
- 如果在家办公需要相关文档的话，给我发电子邮件。
- 你要是准备好了，我来处理电话会议。这样你就能了解项目的最新进展情况。

联系相关人员

- 如果工作中想让我联系其他人，请告诉我。我很乐意帮忙。
- 你想让我通知你的团队什么事情吗？或者让他们电话联系你吗？
- 你想让我联络谁吗？
- 你介意我给你团队成员发电子邮件吗？我知道他们关心你，想知道你的消息。

经常了解情况

无论你决定是发电子邮件还是打电话，以下完美措辞都适用。

- 我想询问一下你的感觉如何？
- 就想知道你的近况。
- 我们想念与你共事的日子，想知道你的情况。
- 近来可好？我们欢迎你重返职场。
- 团队里所有人都渴望你归队，我们想念你。

适当时运用幽默

- 你休假后，我们部门基本上散架了。你何时回来？我们需要你。
- 你的办公桌一直空着，大家都等着你回来。没有你在，我们都感到缺少温暖。

小提示

你该在何时发电子邮件或打电话？对于邮件，收件人可以按自己的节奏理解其内容或者暂时不予考虑，而且邮件不需要收件人答复。他们阅读后，不必立即按下回复键，回复感谢之类的言辞。但是邮件比较随意，交流不多。对于电话这种方式，如果双方关系亲密，熟到可以开玩笑的话，打电话有助于传递温情。与身患重病的同事联系时，具体采用哪种方式？这要从三个方面考虑来确定，即同事的喜好、对方的心情以及你们之间的关系。

员工由于健康原因必须休假

与这种人沟通需要技巧。无论你是对方的朋友、项目经理还是上司。你应该表示同情，同时也要牢记职责。你还要做出专业决策来解决由此造成的工作分工问题。你也得注意在保护隐私前提下通告相关情况。以下完美措辞有助于你在众多因素中保持平衡，维护职场稳定。

员工告知相关消息后

表达个人关心

- 得知你要离职，我很难过。
- 希望你尽快康复。
- 很难过你离开，不过相信你会很快好起来。
- 很抱歉听到这个不幸的消息。我们能如何帮忙?
- 你还好吗?

小提示

无论你的出发点有多好，注意不要过度表达同情。不要做出任何许诺性言论，尤其是书面形式的。一旦出现问题，这些都会对你不利。

错误用语：

- 真糟糕。好好休假，康复后再上班。没问题，我们会帮你处理好一切的，并为你保留原职。
- 病去如抽丝。如果你的休假需要延期的话，我也能理解。
- 这在精神上和身体上都是一次挑战。好在你供职于我们这样的公司，我们有完美的员工医疗保健方案，休假政策也很体贴。

正确用语：

- 请告诉我们医生建议的康复时间。
- 一定要在康复期间照顾好自己。
- 我知道这并不容易，但是这里每个人都渴望尽快听到你康复的好消息。

讨论安排协调事宜

- 医生说你需要多长时间康复？
- 你计划在家办公吗？如果是这样，你认为何时可以开始？
- 你准备在家处理什么业务？
- 你何时能部分恢复工作？完全恢复呢？
- 我们必须弄清你所有的项目清单以及各自的进展情况。最好的做法是什么？
- 我想了解你所有关键项目继任者的情况。你何时方便处理此事？
- 你想参加电话会议的旁听吗？要是参加，我们将非常乐于安排此事。

确定方案

- 这就是我们对未来两个月的期望。
- 这就是从四月份以来我们采用的方案。
- 请告知我们你对此安排的意见。
- 确保我们有你的联系号码。万一我们需要你，给你打电话的最佳时间是……

明确你能公开的内容和需保密的内容

- 我必须告诉别人你要休假。你想让我告诉他们什么？
- 我会告诉你的客户你要休假一段时间。你想让我代写电子邮件吗？完成后让你过目如何？或者你亲自写？
- 大家会问你的情况。我能告诉他们什么？
- 你想让别人知道你的病情吗？要不我只告诉他们你生病去休假了？
- 你知道大家真的很关心你。我能说点什么以免他们过于担心？
- 我能否告诉大家你的私人电子邮箱以便联络？

对于职场中或团队里其他同事的应答

此时你也许很想说出该员工患病的详情，尤其是当其必须在家养病时。但是保密是关键。所以最好还是不要说出病情，而是使用以下完美措辞。

就事论事

● ________ 因病要休假一段时间。不过医生说三四周后我们就可以去看他了。

● ________ 患________疾病。目前他情况还好，但是要休假几周。

● ________ 刚告诉我他要休病假两个月。

● ________ 还要休假，因为……估计秋天归队。

需要时，从健康的角度告知他人相关的影响。

● 这种病不会传染，不用为自己健康担心。

● 这种病会传染。如果你皮肤出现持续疼痛，要及时就诊。

● 该病是否传染，目前连专家都还不清楚。网络上列举了相关健康警示。

● 他很可能是食用了不洁食物而患上了这种病。公司里没有人出现同类问题，我们由此推测餐厅食物质量可靠。

● 这种病不传染，但很可能遗传。你应该找医生做个检查，以便早日排查问题。

讨论协调安排事宜

● 我们必须看项目表，以便分工协作。

● 我们每人分担他的一部分工作，这样就可以全部完工了。

● 我会看看他的工作，把那些不能耽误的分工完成。

● 我有________ 负责的项目清单，其中大多数工作可以放缓一下进度，但是我会给你们部分员工安排些额外工作。下周早些时候通知你们。

● 我有一张任务表，需要帮助________ 完成。他休假了，请查阅后归入你的日程表。

如果有人必须承担主要责任，应确保团队所有成员提供支持。

● ________ 要承担主要责任，他认识其中许多客户。不过，我们都要全力以赴帮忙。

● 很感谢________ 愿意负责。其他人如何帮忙?

● 他休假期间，________ 代为承担了过多责任。要是________ 遇到困难，我们要尽力帮助。

告诉你的同事，你非常感谢他们认真参与。

- 十分感谢你们为此做出的努力。谁也没想到________休假时间会如此长。
- 我知道你们都有大量的工作要做。在________休假期间，你们乐意伸出援手。对此，我感激万分。
- 感谢你们所有人这段时间的帮助。长远看，你们的努力将使每个人受益，也包括我们的客户。
- 十分感谢你们合力帮助。没有你们，我真不敢相信事情会变得有多糟糕。

其他人非议该员工缺勤时应对的措辞

缺勤是身不由己，它并不能表明该员工不负责任。所以，其他人只有接受这个现实。尽量以就事论事的态度来回答。

- ________病了。谁也不想这样，尤其是________本人。所以我们要尽量做好。
- 这是个困难时期。我们必须支持________，直到他康复并重返工作岗位。
- 我们要共同努力，承担更多责任。同时还要避免事态恶化。让我们研究如何做好事情。千万不要抱怨。
- 在这种时候，我不想听到抱怨。我想听到好想法，那些有助于顺利过渡的想法。
- 让我们每人写下一两条帮助________完工的方法，并且大声读出来。然后再共同努力寻找推动进展的最佳方法。

同事的配偶或父母去世

显而易见，正确应对死亡的确很难。失去亲人会令人不知所措，但是生活还得继续。你要体谅同事遭遇的痛苦，同时还要做好协调安排。你的处理方式可分为几个阶段，从亲人去世后一两天到其葬礼结束一两周。以下完美措辞可以助你一臂之力。

刚听说其父 / 母过世

讲明你的消息来源，并分享你了解的或记忆中的相关情况，以此强调你的诚意。

- ________刚告诉我你母亲去世了。得知这个消息，我很难过。你们关系一直十分密切。
- 谢谢你告诉我你父亲去世的消息。我知道他生病有一段时间了。你一定很难过。
- 得知你母亲突然离世，我很难过。这太出乎意料了。
- 刚听说你父亲昨天去世了。你们家庭关系亲密，这对你们全家人的打击一定很大。
- 很难过听说你母亲去世了。我记得去年开会遇见过她。当时她很风趣，精神饱满。
- 很难过得知你父亲的噩耗。他知识渊博，我们曾在你女儿婚礼上见过面，我对他印象深刻。

刚听说其配偶去世

配偶去世影响巨大。根据你们之间的关系，酌情考虑你是否该出面，是否要提供帮助。

- 惊闻……十分悲痛。我时刻挂念你，很乐于提供任何帮助。
- 得悉________去世，甚为悲痛。你和孩子们若需要任何帮助，请告诉我。
- 很难过听说……这是个困难时刻。希望你知道所有人都深表同情。

陈词滥调无益于你表达诚意，还不如致哀悼词。因此要避免使用慰问卡上的套语，尽量具体点。请参见以上例句。

避免以下措辞

- 对你失去亲人致以最深的哀悼。
- 我们与你在一起。
- 愿她安息。
- 听说你痛失亲人，我感到悲痛万分。
- 值此痛失亲人之际，致以哀悼。

悲痛的员工还在家休假，处理其重返岗位事宜

具体提出你的要求，让对方明白你理解其处境。

- 能否告诉我们你重返岗位的时间？不用着急。我们只想了解情况，以便做出最好的安排。
- 我们完全尊重你与家人共处的必要性，但是如果你能明确重返岗位的时间，那对我们会非常有帮助。不过不要着急。
- 我们想念与你共事的日子，能够理解你决定再休假一周。要是想尽快回来的话，请告诉我。
- 我们的员工政策规定你可以休假一周。但是你需要的话，大家都愿意一起帮忙。

查询相关工作材料

- 我知道这对你来说是个困难时刻。我尊重你与家人共处的必要性。如果可能的话，能否告诉我你的电脑密码？我们正在代为完成你的工作，这样能确保你重返工作时顺利过渡。
- 我无意干涉你的隐私，只是想与你交谈几分钟。我必须找到……能否通过电话或邮件告诉我联系你的最佳时间？
- 我知道你现在需要一些个人空间。方便给我发邮件吗？如果想和我电话交谈，请告诉我。

员工由于父母或子女生病需要照顾而耽误工作

家中父母或子女生病是非常令人苦恼的，员工理所当然需要休假。但是在忙于照顾生病家人的同时，员工也会有闲暇时间，可以打电话，能回复电子邮件，也可以在其他方面跟上正常的生活节奏。许多员工珍惜这段时间。他们与同事保持联系，思考自己的独立生活。因此你在向员工表达同情时，不要担心问及其具体的工作时间。

刚刚得知此消息

由于其病症并无大碍，可以表示体谅和祝愿。

- 我希望________尽快康复。
- 很难过听说……祝愿她早日康复。
- ________告诉我________生病了。请转告，我祝他尽快好转。

讨论时间问题

如你所见，前一部分完美措辞很容易。现在你必须询问员工休假的具体时间，但并不是催促他。以下完美措辞适用。

- 你估计休假时间会有多长？
- 你知道何时能送你母亲去养老院？
- 你何时能全职重返工作？
- 照顾你父亲的方案确定之前，你需要离职吗？
- 你认为治疗会持续多久？
- 我们要制定方案，以便团队成员在你离职期间能替补。我知道处理这些事情需要时间，但是你认为休假会多久？

询问员工能否在家办公

你想大概了解员工是否能有时间办公。

- 你考虑过在家里分担一些工作吗？
- 你有空通过电子邮件联络吗？

- 你下午能同我们保持联系吗？以便我们遇到问题或需要建议时，能得到你的帮助。

如果情况并不严重，比如孩子感冒了，此时你推测该员工应该可以在家办公。可以使用推测性言语。

- 要是我们需要帮助的话，该如何联络你？
- 电子邮件和电话，哪种方式联系你更好？
- 你打算把哪个项目带到家中做？

如有可能，确定该员工能否负责具体项目。这样你对其贡献能力有明确的期待。

- 你早晨有时间讨论项目方案吗？
- 你能在周五完成预算吗？
- 你能不能电话联系________，同他合作完成……

小提示

尽量不要让员工连续工作好几个小时。如果中途打断或受到干扰，对方的时间观念会很不明确。结果是该员工声称（也许是真心认为）已经工作了 3 个小时，但是只完成了 1 个小时工作量。当然若该员工是按小时取酬的话就是例外。

你正经历个人困境，工作需要弹性安排

经历个人危机时，你最不愿意去做的就是确定休假策略。但是你不可能简单地不来上班，必须联系上司、同事，也可能是客户。尽可能用一种最专业的方式让他们了解到，你的私人困境目前使生活一团糟。沟通前，弄清你需要的休假时间长短，明确需要他人代替完工的内容。如果需要你配合，告知对方联系的具体时间和次数。

讨论这个主题时，简单介绍你的处境。

- ________生病了，我需要照顾他。
- ________ 离家出走，我需要时间处理此问题。

- 我刚听说……必须飞到________解决问题。
- 我要请假几个月，因为……
- ________的医生刚通知我们，他必须住院，所以我需要请假至少1周。

讨论你的方案，但是不要过于具体，这样你还有灵活度。除此之外，一旦你做出承诺，人们就期望你信守诺言，所以还要留有余地。

错误用语：

- 我会周四早上回来。
- 我每天至少有3小时用在项目上。
- 我每天早上8点整打电话开早会。
- 我会帮助________完成……

正确用语：

- 我将在本周末的某个时间回来。
- 我每天至少工作一两个小时。
- 每天上午能联系到我，如果万一不能参会，克莱尔会转交给我相关记录。
- 我会帮助________完成项目。

有时你并不需要离职，只是要改变工作时间，这种情况下必须明确给出具体时间安排。

错误用语：

- 我的工作时间要减少。
- 我需要不同的工作时间。
- 我尽量按时完成，或者找到替代的方法。
- 不久以后我的上班时间要推后一些。

正确用语：

- 我每周的工作时间只有20小时。

- 以下两周我的工作时间需要调整为上午 10 点到下午 6 点。
- 我将尽力按时完成，或者提醒克莱尔再安排其他人来完成。
- 我 10 点才能上班，这种情况需要持续至少 1 个月。

最好是使用“如果……那么……”的句式来表达，这可以使所有相关人员都清楚能指望你做些什么。

如果……　　　　　　那么……

- 如果周二我不在，那么我会利用周末补上工作。
- 要是我没有接听电话，那么请拨打我手机。
- 如果要进入我邮箱账户，那么请向莎拉询问我的密码。

明确你的联络时间。

- 你可以在清早或下午晚些时候联系我。
- 我能按时完成现有项目，但是回来后才能接手新项目。
- 我只有接下来几周不能全职工作。
- 我需要每天下午 3 点下班。

小提示

尽管同事都很有同情心，不过不要把他们当作密友，不必向其诉苦。你应该告诉对方自己离职或工作日程变更的原因，工作之余再谈论相关私人细节。

你由于个人原因必须离职，但最终可能想重返岗位

人们由于各种原因离职，有人是身体不好；有人要寻求更好的职位；有人想返校充电。这些情况下，他们只要简单告别，祝愿大家一切顺利就行了。但离职后还想返回的话，那就另当别论了。这种离职要精心策划，不要出现你走后业务突然中止或项目退出的情况。你还必须认真说明离职原因，不要让人感到冒犯或使人陷入困境。以下完美措辞即使在你将大门关闭的情况下，也能帮你再将其打开。

总结你对工作的满意之处

具体说明情况，态度要诚恳。确定你对工作的满意之处，表达你的观点。当然具体细节要视你的经历而定，不过你可以这样开头：

- 我很喜欢……
- 感谢你给我……
- 我最感激的是……
- 我刚来……几周后，我……
- 经验告诉我……
- 我最喜欢的一点是……
- 我最爱的是……
- 我最自豪的是……

结束语可以采用以下方式：

- 我真的很喜欢与大家共事。虽然工作强度很大并且总是有不断的挑战，但是我们仍然乐趣无穷。
- 能有机会操作新系统，太棒了。这比我在大学里学到的东西还多。
- 我最自豪的是我们成功处理了麦凯恩公司的账目。多亏我们团队同心协力合作，一切才能进展顺利。
- 我会想念每周二制定策略的那段时间。

切记避免以下缺乏诚意的言辞：

- 谢谢你们的支持。
- 多谢你给我机会。
- 我会记住大家的。
- 我很满意这份工作。

提醒他们你可能会回来：

- 希望有朝一日我能归来，再次与大家共事。
- 虽然目前我有新挑战，但我相信很快会与大家再会。
- 我想以全新的视角，带着不同的经历，重新加入大家的队伍中。

清楚说明离职原因

确保关注未来的积极方面，不要涉及离职的负面原因。

错误说法：

- 我在这儿没有太多长进，需要返校充电。
- 这份工作压力太大，时间太久，我已经耗尽全力了。
- 我不喜欢这儿的人，想躲开他们。
- 工资太少，升职机会太渺茫。

正确说法：

- 我需要返校充电，使自己得到提高。
- 我想减少工作时间，以便有机会调整生活节奏。
- 我想到小企业就职，或者自己当老板。
- 我想在新环境工作，寻求晋升的机会。

指明离职的具体时间

- 我计划于________离职，这样我就有3周时间准备，你们也可找到人接替。
- 我们完成________后，我就离职。这个时间估计会在两周后。
- 我正计划离职过渡，1月到3月我会干兼职。4月1日离职。
- 由于意外地被接受参加一个项目，我必须两周后离职。离职后两周内，我会参加项目讨论，帮助完成未尽事宜。

询问顺利离职的途径

- 我计划离职前做好收尾工作。如果有事需要安排，请通知我。
- 请告诉我如何顺利离职。
- 我走前，如果有事需要帮忙，请通知我。我要在________那天离开办公室。如果提前通知我公事的话，我一定完成。
- 我想尽量多完成工作。由于有些工作几个月后才到期，我会进行协调，以便继任者顺利适应。您还需要我做些什么？

写告别信

写信，向那些给予你最大帮助的人表示感谢，还要向那些关系密切的合作伙伴致谢。内容要尽量显得精美，这样打印出来不仅一目了然，而且能表达心意。不过发邮件也不错，因为你只需要一两行内容就能起到很好的效果。如果你重返岗位，大家同样会对你有好感。邮件要内容具体、富有诚意。具体内容取决于你的经历。当然，可采用以下方式：

- 十分感谢你的午夜提案，还有那些让我捧腹大笑的笑话。
- 很感激你专心致志帮助我处理数据系统，我从中受益匪浅。无论以后从事何种工作，我都将牢记在心。
- 祝愿你们顺利完成麦凯恩公司项目，我相信你们会一如既往出色完工。
- 很怀念与你共进午餐的时光，但愿以后我们能经常联系。

Part Four

When Personal Tragedies Flare Up at Work

The workplace is about professional and nonpersonal relationships. Sure, we talk about our kids, our aspirations, and what we did for vacation, but we don't get into great detail. That's not the point of being at work—or of having work relationships. But now and then, you have no option but to mix the personal and professional, especially when a colleague has suffered a tragedy.

Communicating about these issues is harder to do than most people think. You have to mix emotional factors with logistical ones. You must slow down and consider someone else's feelings or life situation . . . without missing deadlines or slowing the pace of work. And you must be sympathetic without being syrupy or inappropriate. It is a hard balance to achieve, indeed. So what should you do? Read through these pointers. Then we'll look at difficult situations and perfect phrases for addressing them.

- **Show, don't tell.** Objectively describe the event that is occurring rather than explain how horrible, sad, or mind-boggling the situation is. This is the fundamental difference between showing and telling. When telling, you explain the situation from your point of view and hope people agree. When showing, you let people see the situation for themselves and come up with the right conclusions.

Notice the difference here—you'll see more as you review the perfect phrases in this section:

Show: He needs back surgery that will keep him in traction for a few weeks.

Tell: He has to undergo painful and exhausting surgery to his back.

- **Be precise about the future.** If your coworker is ill, say that you or others will fill in during his or her absence. When contacting others, tell them how long your coworker will be out and specifically how they can help.

Don't: We'll need to take on ____'s tasks while she is out of work.

Do: We'll need to e-mail the billings and check for delayed payments for the next two days.

● Comment only on what's apparent. It's critical that you give your coworker the right to privacy and the space to express—or not express—his or her feelings. And yes, it's always nice to sympathize; just sympathize in an appropriately limited way:

Don't: I'm sure that's really uncomfortable, especially when you go to the bathroom.

Do: I'm sorry to hear you're in pain.

A Colleague Is Diagnosed with a Serious Illness

This situation may be the most sensitive of them all. A colleague learns difficult news that brings promises of pain and, probably, mandatory time off. You don't want to pry, but you don't want to seem insensitive or uncaring. So here's what you do.

Express Concern

Chances are, your colleague is nervous and, quite possibly, feeling the need for privacy. So use these perfect phrases to address the situation—then let your colleague talk or not, depending on what he or she feels most comfortable doing.

When Someone Else Told You About the Illness

● ____ told me you were ill. I hope you're not feeling too badly.

● I just heard that you were feeling badly and wanted to check in.

● Are you feeling okay? I just heard you were diagnosed with ____.

● I don't want to pry or embarrass you, but I heard you were unwell and wanted to express my concern.

When Your Colleague Told You About His or Her Illness

● I'm sorry to hear that.

- What a surprise. Thank you for telling me.
- That's too bad. How do you feel?
- So sorry to hear about the diagnosis.

When Appropriate, Offer Encouragement

- You look so healthy, though. I'm sure you can beat it.
- You've always taken such good care of yourself; I know you have the power to resist it.
- I know you're smart enough to get the right help to overcome this illness.
- I've heard that doctors have made major strides in curing this illness.
- They have all sorts of new medications that can help.

Quick tip

If you know someone who contracted the illness and survived, you can mention it. Knowing others have gone through the difficult situation can be helpful.

Offer Support

Often, open-ended offers of support help people feel cared for but not intruded on:

- Can I help in any way?
- What can I do for you?
- Anything you need?
- How can I assist you?

Yet they can also sound insincere. So whenever possible, be specific:

- Since you won't be able to drive, let me know if I can take you to work.
- If you need me to cover for you in the mornings, just let me know.
- I can complete the report if you're not up to it.
- Just e-mail me if you need any of the office files while you're working at home.
- I can arrange conference calls when you're ready, so you can keep abreast of the project.

Ask Whom You Can Tell

● If you want me to contact anyone at work, let me know. I'll be happy to do so.

● Do you want me to tell your team anything or have them call you?

● Whom would you like me to contact for you?

● Would you mind if I e-mailed the members of your team? I know they care about you and would want to hear.

Check In from Time to Time

Whether you send an e-mail or call on the telephone is up to you. These perfect phrases work in both instances:

● I was checking to see how you were feeling.

● Just wanted to know how you're doing.

● We miss you here at work and wanted to check in.

● So what's going on—we want you back in the office.

● Everyone on the team wants to know when you're coming back. We miss you.

Use Humor When Appropriate

● Since you've been out, our department has basically fallen apart. When will you be back? (We need you!)

● We have this little vacuum at your desk—everyone's waiting for you to get back and fill it. (The breeze is making us cold!)

Quick tip

When should you initiate an e-mail or a phone call? E-mails give your audience a chance to absorb the message—or leave it aside—at their own pace. Besides, e-mails don't require anything from the recipients. They read it and aren't obligated to respond outside of hitting the reply button and saying something like "Thanks." Still, e-mails can seem less formal and less interactive. As for the telephone, if you have a strong or joking relationship, calls can help draw a warm and important connection. Which you use when contacting an employee with a serious illness depends on the employee's preference, his or her state of mind, and your relationship.

An Employee Must Take Leave Because of a Health Problem

Communicating with this person—whether you're a friend, project manager, or boss—can be tricky. You need to be sympathetic without yielding beyond the call of duty. You need to make professional decisions about how to distribute work because of highly personal matters. And you need to spread the word without breaking confidentiality. These perfect phrases will help you strike a balance between all these factors to keep the workplace stable.

What to Say When the Employee Gives You the News

Express Personal Concern

- I'm really sorry to hear that you'll be out.
- I hope you recover quickly.
- Sorry you won't be here; hopefully, you'll be feeling great soon.
- I'm sorry to hear about this problem. How can we help?
- Are you feeling okay?

Remember

Be careful not to overdo the sympathy, in spite of your best intentions. And don't make any promissory statements, especially in writing. Should problems arise, these will work against you.

Don't

- How awful—please, take as much time as you need to recover. We'll fill in for you, no problem, and your place will be here when you return.
- Health problems can really be debilitating. I'll understand if you need to take a leave for weeks longer than you predict.
- This is tough mentally and physically. Good thing you work for a company like ours that has such a good health plan and understanding leave policies.

Do

- Just let us know how much time your doctor says you'll need to recover.
- Be sure to take really good care of yourself while you're off recovering.
- I know this isn't easy, but everyone here is eager for a fast recovery.

Discuss Logistical Matters

● How much time did the doctor say you need to recover?

● Are you planning to work from home? If so, when do you think you can start?

● What kinds of work will you be able to do from your house when you're ready?

● When do you think you'll be able to return to work part time? Full time?

● We need to get a list of all your projects and your progress in each of them. What is the best way to do this?

● I'd like some input about who should fill in on your key projects. When will be the best time for you to do this?

● Would you like to listen in to our meetings on a conference call? If so, I'll be happy to arrange that.

Settle on a Plan

● So here's what we can expect over the next two months . . .

● Here's our game plan through April . . .

● Let me know what you think of this arrangement . . .

● Make sure we have your contact numbers, in case we need you, and the best times to call . . .

Determine What You Can and Cannot Say to Other People

● I need to tell people that you'll be out. What would you like me to tell them?

● I'd like to tell your clients that you'll be gone for a while. Would you like me to write an e-mail on your behalf and show you before it goes out? Or would you like to write one yourself?

● People will be asking questions. How much detail can I give them?

● Do you want people to know that you have _____, or should I just tell them that you're sick and leave it at that?

● People here really care about you, as you know. So what can I tell them so they don't worry too much?

● Can I give people your home e-mail for personal correspondences?

What to Say to Others in the Workplace or on Your Team

Yes, you may be aching to give away details about the employee's ailment, especially when it underscores that the employee really does need to stay home recovering. But confidentiality is key, so better not. Instead, use the perfect phrases.

Be Factual

- _____ will be out for a while because he is ill. The doctor says we should see him in three to four weeks, though.
- _____ contracted _______. The situation looks good, but she will need to take a few weeks off.
- _____ just told me he will need to be out on sick leave for the next two months.
- _______ needs to take another leave because of _____. We expect her to return in the fall.

When appropriate, let others know how they may be affected from a health perspective:

- This isn't contagious, so you won't have to worry about your own health.
- This is contagious, so if you notice a skin irritation that won't go away, contact your doctor.
- Whether or not this is contagious, no one seems to know—even specialists. You can find a list of warning signs on the Web.
- It's possible she contracted the illness from eating bad food. Since no one in the company has this problem, though, we assume the food in the cafeteria is fine.
- As you know, the problem isn't contagious and is, most likely, hereditary. You should go to your doctor for a screening, though, to detect any problems early.

Discuss Logistical Matters

- We need to look at his project list to divide up responsibilities.
- All of us need to take one of her assignments, and we should cover them all.
- I'll review his responsibilities and assign whichever ones can't wait for his return.
- I have a list of _____'s projects. Most of the steps here can wait, but I'll need to

assign some of you extra tasks to cover. You'll hear from me early next week.

● I have a list of assignments that will help cover for _____ when she is out. Please review them and build them into your schedule of events.

If one person will have to share the bulk of the responsibility, be sure all the members of your team know they must provide support:

● _____ must take on these responsibilities since she shares many of these clients. However, we should all be available to pitch in.

● I appreciate _____'s willingness to take on these responsibilities. How can the rest of us help?

● I know that _____ has more than his share of responsibilities to cover for _____ while she is out. So if _____ is in a crunch, let's all agree to pitch in any way we can.

Let your coworkers know that you appreciate their efforts to pitch in:

● I really appreciate your helping out with this. No one expected that _____ would be out this long.

● I know you guys are swamped with work as it is. So I doubly appreciate your willingness to help ___ while he is out.

● Thank you all for being so helpful at this time. In the long run, everyone including our customers will benefit from your efforts.

● Thanks so much for pitching in. I can't even imagine how bad things would get if you hadn't.

What to Say When Others Protest the Employee's Absence

The absence is not optional or a sign of the employee's irresponsibility. So everyone else will simply have to live with it. State this as matter-of-factly as you can:

● _____ is sick. No one asked for that to happen, least of all _____. So we have to do our best.

● This is a difficult time, and we must get behind _____ until he is well enough to return.

● We need to pull together to take on additional responsibilities without letting other things slide. So let's look at what we can do to keep things going, rather than complain.

● I don't want to hear complaints, at this time. I would like to hear ideas, though, about what we can do to make this transition easier.

● Why doesn't everyone write down one or two ways you can help fill in for ____ and read them aloud. Then we'll work together to find the best steps for moving ahead.

A Colleague's Partner or Parent Dies

Obviously, death is something no one can respond to in quite the right way. The loss can be overwhelming, and yet life needs to go on. You need to acknowledge the pain your colleague is confronting—while clarifying logistical issues. How you do this can occur in stages—from a day or so after the death occurred to a week or so from the funeral. Here are some perfect phrases to help.

When First Learning About the Death of a Parent

Mention how you learned about the event, and share whatever knowledge or memories you have to underscore your sincerity:

● ____ just told me that your mother passed away. I was so sorry to hear about it. I know the two of you were quite close.

● Thank you for letting me know about your father's passing. I understand that he was sick for some time; still, this must be difficult for you.

● Sorry to hear that your mother passed away so suddenly. This must be a terrible shock.

● I just learned that your father passed away yesterday. I know you were such a close family; this must be a real shock to you all.

● So sorry to hear that your mother died. I remember meeting her at the conference last year. She was a funny and spirited woman.

● Sorry to hear about your father. He was a learned man: I was most impressed when I met him at your daughter's wedding.

When First Learning About the Death of a Partner

Because the death of a spouse or partner can have an immediately devastating effect, make yourself as present and available as is appropriate for your relationship:

● I was surprised and saddened to learn about ____. Please know I'm thinking about you constantly and will be happy to help in any way I can.

● ________, I was so sorry to learn that ____ passed away. If there is anything I, or anyone in my family, can do for you and the kids, please let me know.

● I was so sad to hear about _____. I know this must be hard: I hope you realize everyone here feels for you.

Clichés diminish the sincerity of any message—none quite so much as a condolence note. So avoid some of the clichés you might find on a greeting card, and opt for the specifics, as you can see in the examples above.

Phrases to Avoid

● My deepest condolences for your loss.

● Our thoughts are with you.

● May she rest in peace.

● My deepest sorrow for your loss.

● My sympathies at this great time of loss.

When Addressing Return-to-Work Issues When the Grieving Person Is Still at Home

Be specific about what you need, and let them know that you understand:

● Can you let us know about when you'll be returning to work? There is no hurry. We just need to know so we can best accommodate you.

● I want you to know we respect your need to be with your family. If you have a sense of when you'll return to work, that would be helpful to us. But please, no rush.

● We all miss you at work but understand if you need to take another week off. Just let us know if you want to come back sooner.

● As you know, our employee policy states that you get a week of leave. But everyone here is willing to pitch in if you need extra time.

When Asking for Information About Materials at Work

● I know this is a hard time for you and respect your need to be with your family. If possible, could you tell me the password for your computer? We are covering for you so when you return to work, the transition back will be smooth.

- I don't want to intrude on your privacy but was hoping we could talk for a few minutes. I need to find ____________. Could you give me a call or e-mail about the best time for me to call you?
- I know this is a time when you'll want privacy. Do you think you could e-mail me? If you would like to speak on the phone, just let me know.

An Employee Must Miss Work Because a Parent or Child Is Sick and Requires Attention

Having a sick child or parent is traumatic and most certainly a valid reason for an employee to take time off work. But through the back-and-forth of caring for the sick family member, the employee will also have reprieves: time to make a call, answer e-mails, and otherwise catch up with life. Many employees value this time; they can connect with peers and think about their own, independent lives. So while you obviously need to be empathetic, don't be afraid to ask how much time, if any, an employee can dedicate to work.

When First Hearing the News

Because the person is sick, but not mortally ill, express understanding and hope:

- I hope ____ gets better soon.
- Sorry to hear about _____. Hopefully, she will be up and about soon.
- ______ told me that _____ has been sick. Tell him I said to hurry up and get well.

When Discussing Timing

As you can see, the last set of perfect phrases is easy, if not obvious. But now you have to ask how long the employee will be out, without actually rushing him or her. These perfect phrases should help:

- Do you have a sense of how much time you'll need to be away?
- Do you know when you'll be able to get your mother into a nursing home?
- Do you know when you will be able to return to work full time?
- Will you need to be out of work until plans to care for your father are

established?

- How long do you suppose the treatment will last?
- We need to make plans so members of the team can fill in while you're gone. I know these things can take time, but how long do you think you'll be absent?

When Asking Whether the Employee Can Work from Home

You may need to ask whether the person can devote time to work in a general sense:

- Think you can help us out while you're at home?
- Will you be available through e-mail?
- Do you think you can contact us in the afternoons in case we have questions or need some advice?

If the situation isn't dire, such as a child has a cold, you may use assumptive language, where you assume the person will work from home:

- When will you be available if we need help?
- What is the best way to reach you—by e-mail or phone?
- Which project will you be taking home with you?

When possible, see if the person can commit to concrete projects. This will put clear expectations on how much, or little, of a contribution you can expect.

- Will you have any time in the morning to discuss the project plan?
- Could you try to complete the budget by Friday?
- Can you work with ____ over the phone to finish ______?

Quick tip

Try not to get the person to commit to a certain number of hours. If interrupted or otherwise distracted, he or she may not have a clear sense of time. Then the person will (honestly) claim he or she worked for three hours but only completed one hour's worth of work. The exception, of course, is when the person is paid an hourly fee.

You Are Experiencing Personal Problems and Need Flexibility at Work

When enduring a personal crisis, the last thing you want is to determine strategies for taking time off work. But you can't simply not show up. So you need to contact your boss, colleagues, and possibly your clients, letting them know in the most professional way possible that a personal issue is, essentially, mucking up your life. Be clear before you start about how much time you'll need; what other people must do to fill in for you; and when you will be available in terms of hours and times of day, should they need help.

When introducing the subject, explain the situation—you can be general:

- ______ is sick, and I need to take care of him.
- ______ has left the family, and I need some time to work things out.
- I just learned that ________ and will have to fly to ______ to sort things out.
- I'll need to take a leave of absence for a few months because______.
- ______'s doctor just told us that she needs to go into the hospital, so I'll need to take at least a week off.

Discuss your plans, but don't be overly specific so you have flexibility. Besides, once you've made a promise, people will expect you to stick with it. So don't get boxed in.

Don't

- I will be back on Thursday morning.
- I can devote at least three hours a day to projects.
- I will call every morning promptly at 8:00 for the morning meeting.
- I will help ______ finish the ______.

Do

- I will be back sometime at the end of the week.
- I can devote at least an hour or two a day.
- I'll try to be in touch every morning. If I miss the morning meeting, Claire can forward me the notes.
- I will help _____ with the project.

Sometimes you won't need time off—just different hours. In this case, you really do need to be specific:

Don't

- I will work less time.
- I need to keep different hours.
- I will try to make my deadlines or figure out alternatives.
- For the foreseeable future, I will need to arrive late for work.

Do

- I will work 20 hours a week.
- I need to work from 10:00 to 6:00 for the next two weeks.
- I'll do my best to make deadlines or alert Claire, who can reassign them to someone else.
- For at least a month, I will need to arrive at work at 10:00.

It's always helpful to send an "if-then" message, so all those involved know what they can expect from you:

If . . .　　　　　　　　　　　　then . . .

- If I am out on Tuesday, then I will make up the work at the end of the week.
- If I don't answer my phone, then try calling my cell.
- If you need to get into my e-mail account, then ask Sarah for my password.

Set boundaries on your availability:

- You can reach me in the early mornings and late afternoons.
- I will be able to complete the existing projects on schedule but can't take any new ones until I return.
- I will be able to work part-time hours only for the next few weeks.
- I will need to leave at 3:00 every afternoon.

Quick tip

Even though your coworkers seem sympathetic, don't treat them as confidantes, telling them about the miseries of your life. Instead, trust them with information that will explain your absence or altered work schedule, and save the personal details for conversations after work.

You Must Leave Your Job for Personal Reasons but May Want to Return Eventually

People leave their jobs for many reasons. They get burned out. Find better positions. Return to school. In these cases, they can simply say good-bye and wish everyone the best. But the plot shifts when you're leaving a job but might want to come back later. Your departure must be carefully planned: no sudden exits and dropped projects in your wake. And you must do a good enough job of explaining why you're leaving so no one feels insulted or stranded. These perfect phrases will keep the doors open, even when you close them.

Say What You Like About the Job

Be specific and sincere. Determine what you really did like about the job, and express it. Obviously, the specifics depend on your experience, but your openings may start like this:

- I really enjoyed . . .
- Thank you for giving me . . .
- What I most appreciated was . . .
- When I arrived I was . . . , but after a few weeks, I . . .
- The experience taught me that . . .
- My favorite aspect was . . .
- The best part for me was . . .
- I am proudest of . . .

Or the final statement may say something like this:

- I've really enjoyed working with all of you—the energy was so high and the demands were constant, but we still had fun!

● The opportunity to work on new systems was amazing—I think I learned more than I did in college.

● I am proudest of the way we handled the McCain account. Everything went so smoothly thanks to our great teamwork.

● I'm really going to miss those strategy sessions on Tuesday.

Just avoid insincere-sounding expressions like these:

● Thank you for your support.

● Thank you for the opportunities.

● I will always remember all of you.

● I derived a great deal of satisfaction from this job.

Remind them that you'd like the option to return:

● I hope that someday I can return and work with you again.

● Although I am taking on new challenges, I see all of you in my future, sooner than you might think!

● I'd love to return with my new insights and experiences to participate in the team again.

Explain Why You Need to Leave in Clear and Understandable Terms

Make sure you focus on the positive aspects of what's ahead and not the negative side of why you need to go.

Don't

● I'm not getting enough stimulation here and need to go back to school.

● I'm totally burned out by the pressure and long hours you require.

● I find the people impossible and want to escape.

● The pay structure and promotion opportunities are too small.

Do

● I want the stimulation that I can get by returning to school.

● I need to work fewer hours and have a chance to pace myself.

● I'd like to work for a smaller business or even work for myself.

● I'd like to work in an environment where I can grow into new and higher positions.

Be Precise About the Timing of Your Exit

● I plan to leave on _____. This will give us three weeks to prepare for my exit and for you to start finding a replacement.

● I will leave after we complete _____, which I expect will be in about two weeks.

● My plan is to transition out. I will go to part time from January through March. I plan to leave on April 1.

● Because I was unexpectedly accepted into the program, I must leave in two weeks. I will be available to discuss projects and pitch in on unfinished work for two weeks after that.

Ask What You Can Do to Make Your Departure Easier

● I plan to tie up any loose ends before I leave. If you have anything in particular that needs my attention, please let me know.

● Please let me know how I can help make my departure easier.

● If you need anything in particular from me before I go, just let me know. I will be cleared out of the office on _____. If you give me ample advance notice, I'll be sure to complete the job.

● I am going to complete as many of my assignments as possible. Since some weren't due for a few months, I'll organize them so my replacement can easily jump in. Is there anything else you want me to do?

Send Good-Bye Notes

Send individuals notes thanking people who helped you most or with whom you established strong working relationships. A hard-copy note is always nice: it's tangible and shows thought. However, an e-mail is better than nothing. You only need a line or two. They'll think well of you, should you return for a job. Be specific and sincere. The actual content depends on your experience, of course, but might look like this:

- Thanks so much for helping with those midnight proposals and for making me laugh with all those jokes I won't mention here!
- All that time you devoted to helping me manage the data system really helped. I'll take that learning with me no matter what I finally do.
- I wish you the best with the McCain project. I know, as usual, you'll do a great job.
- I'll really miss our lunches—hopefully, we'll connect now and then for a few more.

第五章

遭遇违抗和怠工

是的，工作已经够难了，还得应对他人的恶意行径，诸如恶语中伤和消极怠工，这些只会使工作更难。但是，不同于其他困境沟通，此时你的应对可能会有法律方面的隐患。你永远不会知道哪些内容可能会使你面临指控，或者会使你不得不花钱请律师解决问题。所以，在你写任何文字材料时都要牢记以下几点：从自我保护、处事策略，以及最重要的一点——司法防范方面按最坏的情况考虑。

- **对每一件事留档。**一定要使用电子邮件复述每一次重要的沟通，并且将其保留几年以上。你永远不会知道麻烦何时会找上门，即使是看上去已经解决了的问题也可能会有麻烦。哪怕是电话交谈或者面谈，也要在随后用电子邮件重述讨论的主要内容。

- **寻找证人。**要有证人，尤其是在讨论极端恶劣的行为时，更要确保这一点。当你提及证人时可以这样说："当我们与约尔谈话时你说过……"或者是以自己的话来记录。无论如何把邮件抄送给某人，不管是老板、律师还是高级专家，总会有所帮助。

- **使用客观语言。**一定要使用正确、具体的词语来描述，不要参杂任何个人情感。例如，不要说："你当众攻击我。"这很容易被对方抵赖掉："不，我没有。"应该这样表达："在19日的会议上你说我'太蠢了，脑子不开窍'以及其他一些攻击性的话。"如果有人大叫大嚷的话，可以加一些客观的说明，比如："有几位顾客问卡尔这样喧哗是想干什么？"

- **要明确自己想要达到的目的。**你为一桩不适当的或者是起负面作用的行为发送一份信息当然是想得到回应，那么这一回应具体是什么呢？是想让他们停止某一行为？离开某一项目？还是被解雇？或是要求其付一笔账（包括利息）？搞清楚自己真正想要的是什么，然后以书面形式表达出来，否则你就只是在发泄而已。

- **不要虚言恫吓。**当你很愤怒或者是已经对棘手的难题不胜其烦时，经常会忍不住进行威胁，扬言要找律师、向行业协会或消费者协会举报或者是采取其他行动。注意：如果你不是当真想这样做的话，就不要虚言恫吓。你可能是想让对方害怕，但是相反，他们很可能真的会去找律师。

持续的消极对抗和抱怨削弱了团队的士气和精力

消极对抗行为（尤其是全体行为）有致命的危害。你无法对结果进行预测，无法制定策略，也不知该信任谁。所以，你的主要任务就是控制局面，同时在分配任务、明确业务关系和行动方面要尽量表达清楚，不容置疑。

当消极对抗的同事在某一项目上暗中阻碍你

要集中精力关注项目而不要关注自身，即使你认为这些消极对抗行为是针对你本人的。

首先，用客观的、可检验的语言描述这些消极行为。

- 我们让你周五完成________，但是你没有完成这一任务，并且没有事先告诉我或者是其他同事。
- 在上午 9 点的电话中你说已经准备好了，当我到达时却发现你还没有准备。
- 你告诉我说准备每天用 4 个小时做________，但是记录表明你甚至一次都没有做。
- 在项目计划中规定你应该在________时完成________，现在你却宣称自己还没有开始那项工作。

然后，表明这些行为对团队产生了什么影响。

● 结果我们不能按计划完成________，这将会引起资金流转的问题，在你完成那些步骤之前我们无法结账。

● 我已经无法和客户一起快速、高效地工作了，这使得客户很不满意，并且发邮件向老板反映。这些情况你都清楚。

● 我们无法做到________而那是我们共同计划好的方案。这耽误了我们好几周，也许好几个月的时间。

● 我们中的 3 个人不得不紧急投入进来让一切回到正轨上。

下一步再讲述你对团队的期望。

● 你必须完成________和________来赶上进度，我们将在周二的会议上跟踪你的进展。

● 你必须给客户发送一份道歉声明，并且承诺采取措施解决已经造成的问题，请把该邮件抄送给我和老板。

● 你必须于________时提供……

● 你必须马上开始行动并且给团队中的所有人发送运行记录。

当同事的闲话损害了你在公司的声望

直接和他们面谈，明确地告诉对方你希望他们停止这一行为。

● 我知道你对我的私生活方面颇有微词，这种人身攻击不适合职场，你不能再这样做了。

● 据办公室里很多人反映，你说过……这样做让你我都颜面扫地，你必须停止这一做法。

● 对我的私生活随你怎么想，但你不能去和别人议论。

● 如果你对我的工作方式有意见，可以直接对我说。

有时，消极对抗的同事为了损害你的权威，会告诉你一些别人对你的负面评价。这种做法很伤人，是不职业的，也不得体。告诉他们别再这样做。

● 请别再告诉我说________不喜欢我的着装方式，这与工作无关。

● 你好像知道很多别人对我的个人评价，这使我觉得你正在背后议论我。这很不职业，你不能再这样做。

● 我并不关心________或者是别人对我的……的想法，所以用不着告诉我这些。

员工采用消极对抗的方式损害了你威信，要对其进行制约。

● 一旦我们决定了……就没什么可讨价还价的了。

● 如果你对我的管理方式有意见，那就安排一次会议专门讨论此事。

● 我知道你们中的很多人对此项目有疑虑，不过你们私下讨论很不利于工作，我们应该开个会一起讨论一下。

● 如果你们对项目有任何问题，可以直接反映给我或其他团队领导，我们会给予正确的回应。

在这些话语之后附上一个客观的例子，说明他们是如何损害了你的威信。

面对一群牢骚满腹的员工

● 从现在起我们只讨论能够做什么，而不是不能做什么。

● 在活动挂图上把你们的牢骚写在一列，把解决方案写在另一列。

● 大家分成几组，起草一个方案谈谈你们打算如何解决这些问题。

● 你们认为什么是最好的解决方法？

如果没有人发言响应就散会，并且告诉他们把想法写下来交给你。

合伙人想要窃取你的项目

也许你的合伙人认为他们更有资格做这个项目，或者是合同中的某个漏洞使他们有机可乘。不管怎样，只要该项目属于你，并且你已经投入很大精力了，那就用同样的精力来守住它。可采用如下完美措辞。

意识到有人要窃取你的项目

表明你是如何知道该人意图的，并且提出证据证明该项目属于你。二者的顺序并不重要，只要确定相关细节能证明自己的观点。

● ________告诉我说你正打算……该项目，我们的合同规定了我方负责此项工作，正如以下段落所示（直接引用该段落）……

● 我最近听说你打算……在12月6日的会议上客户请我负责此项目，并且我们已经启动了相关工作。我有电子邮件可以证明这一点，如果你需要的话我可以把它们发给你。

● 根据我们之间的协议，我方从2010年夏季负责________，如果你想让自己的员工加入此项目，请直接与我联系，我们将讨论是否有这方面的需求。

● 根据我们2007年4月达成的共识，你是我们公司的一个分包商，所以你在此项目上采取任何行动之前都必须先与我方沟通。

提醒客户或者项目管理者

态度要友好，并且要就事论事，不应该使客户卷入你与第三方之间令人不快的纠纷中。

● 仅此通知您，根据您6月14日的要求，我们已经启动了________我方刚刚获知________也在进行同样的步骤，先向您汇报一下，以免我们双方进行重复性的劳动。

● 我昨天与________通过话，显然________正准备……我方已经同意承担那一方面的项目，并且已派专家到场，我们将继续推进该项目。

● 如您所知，我们的项目计划准备就绪并且开展了前两个阶段的工作。________可能有他们自己的计划，但是，半途转入此项目将耗费大量的时间和成本。

如果有帮助的话，可以寻求你方客户的支持。

● 根据我们在团队会议上所讨论的……您希望我方于________时完成……若这并非您的真实想法，请通知我们。

● 根据我们双方的合同，我的团队负责……________却告知我们他正准备接手此项工作。能否请您澄清一下？以便我方继续进行工作。

● 关于由谁来负责……的问题出现了几个疑问，能请您确认一下吗？

提醒你的同事和员工注意此事

● 如你们所知，我方已经向________提供________服务将近两年了。这是我们的合同，如果你们发现有人试图接手此项业务的话，请通知我。

● 我们是________项目的主承包商，这是我方于2003年通过激烈的竞标获得的。合同的有效期还有两年，如果你从任何其他人处收到了相关指示的话，请马上通知我。

● 根据我近期收到的一封电子邮件，________正打算参与________项目。我们已经在做此项目了，而________并未获得授权这样做，如果情况有什么变化请通知我。

你的公司或合伙人向客户谎报工作量以获得更多的业务

毫无疑问，并不是所有人都适合站出来警告别人，尤其是提醒对方注意自己的公司行为。但是你并不需要采取如此激烈的行为，只要让你的同事知道他们正在犯错就足以使其悬崖勒马。以下完美措辞将有助于此，并且可使你避免惹上麻烦。

就某一方案提供反馈意见

● 这个方案看上去不错，只是第一行有一些问题。我们以往做……从未需要如此多的时间，应该可以减去两天。

● 如果去除……和……的话，我们可以把服务时间缩短一半。这样对结果毫无影响，而且客户会对这样的进度非常满意。

● 在我们以前的方案中，只需要________时间来做________如果没有充分理由的话，最好还是提供我们的例行安排。

● 我觉得这一方案确实要价过高了，我们的目标应该是……这样对客户才公平。

在会上讨论某一项目

- 我觉得应该讨论一下“工作范围”一栏中的真实成本。
- 伙计们，干得不错。不过，我觉得我们对客户要价过高了。
- 我知道，我们偶尔会加入一些“填料”。是否可以给对方一个价格范围，并且尽力保持低价格呢?
- 这一方案看起来并不公平，我们的等级并未提高，而此客户却要比其他人多付 25% 的费用。

确定如何给客户开出当周账单

直截了当，把你的意见集中在单项支出上，要针对单项的数据和日期。当然，具体讲话内容取决于你所处的实际环境，但大体来说可以采用以下方式。

- 我们要求客户支付两次工作午餐会议的费用，分别在 5 月 10 日和 21 日。这两次工作午餐我都参加了，但这两次午餐会议都没有讨论与此客户相关的业务。
- 我们只在此项目上花费了两个小时，即 1 月 10 日下午 3 点至 5 点。
- 如果我的记录有误的话请指正，但是，我确信龙尼没有参加 5 月 1 日的报告会，所以我们不能在账单上加入他的工作时间。
- 我邀请客户在 12 月 30 日与我方员工会面，只是表示一种友好的姿态，而不是一次工作会面。所以，不应该让客户为此付费。

供应商未能提供所承诺的服务

在这种情况下，文件是最有用的了，你必须以文件的形式记录下你们之前达成的所有共识（无论对方是否履行了）以及相关的证据。当服务进行时，也要将其记录下来。在给供应商发邮件或者与之进行讨论时，要使用这些记录作为证据来支持你的观点。

指出问题

- 在合同中贵方承诺将提供……但我方从未获得此项服务。
- 贵方承诺将于________时提供……我方接受此项服务的时间已经比预定日期推迟了两天，并且其间还中断了3次。
- 在双方的协议中，你方承诺将指定________和________为我方提供帮助，但他们从未与我方取得联系。
- 贵方承诺正在负责我方账目的________会帮助我方进行……但________否认这是他的职责。

若问题持续存在

- 签署服务协议时，我承诺将为以下服务……支付……但我只收到了以下服务（列出这些服务的内容及日期）……如今贵方却要求我为所有的服务付费。
- 正如我在5月14日所发电子邮件中描述的那样，我仍然没有收到________，而且你所提供的……还有以下问题……我在5月1日那个星期里多次与________联系，但至今没有任何改善。
- 从8月14日与贵方签署服务协议起，我遇到了以下问题……我已经将每一项都详细记录下来了，如果你需要的话我可以将这些记录发给你。

确实收到了所要求的产品或服务，但质量很差

- 你发给我的……有如下问题……
- 贵方员工按协议提供了服务，但是他们并没有回复我关于……的电话。________没有修好，它从________到________一直不能正常工作。
- 贵方所提供的服务一直都有问题，尤其是对于……我已经就此问题给你们发了邮件，如果需要的话，我可以把复件发给你。
- 你方并没有按合同提供________或________而且，________还有以下问题……我已经多次在电话和邮件中列举了相关问题，并且都已经做了记录。

你被要求为自己不想要的服务付费

● 自________起，我开始收到你们的________服务。但是，这并不是我要求的，尽管我曾要求你们停止这一服务，但你们却没有停止。

● 请不要再给我提供________我从未要求此项服务，也不会为此付费。

● 我刚刚意识到，贵方在我正常的账单中加入了________，但是贵方并未告知我们要为此额外付费。请立即停止此项服务，并且从我的每月账单中将此费用去除。

● 我的助手通知我说，贵方正在依据……向我方收取________的费用。而我方从未要求此项服务，也不打算接受。

小提示

有时你希望对劣质服务要求赔偿。如果是这样的话，你知道该要求些什么吗？该在何时提出要求？我的建议是让对方先提出，理由如下：你要求的可能会比他们愿意提供的还要少，这样你就没办法再多要了。而如果他们提供的比你预想的少时，你总还可以要求追加。

以下是一些用于要求赔偿的完美措辞。记住：要公平，同时态度要坚定。

● 请告知我，你们打算如何为这次错误向我提供补偿。

● 你们将来打算如何处理这些问题？

● 你们准备如何补偿我的这些差额？

● 这些问题使我偏离了项目目标，你们打算如何解决？

● 这些问题让我的损失很大，我可以给你发一份明细表，详细记述由此带来的花销。你必须就这些额外费用向我提供补偿。

大批员工突然跳槽到竞争对手的公司

他们的确走了，这些曾经热爱你和你的公司的员工跳槽去了竞争对手一方。如何阻止进一步的人员流失？而且，这些人走了以后你该怎么办？还有，该如何处理留下来的员工的士气问题？在此已经准备好了一些完美措辞，但是，首先要检查一下你本人的士气问题。另外，请记住，每一个混乱的事件都是一个改进的机会。

营造团队归属感

大家都知道有人跳槽了，与其否认这一点还不如讨论一下这个问题，甚至可以借此机会打造一个更加强大的团队。可以采用以下措辞。

- 是的，有些员工跳槽了，我们很想念他们。但是，这也是一次很好的机会，借此机会我们可以为所有人重新设定全新的、更高的目标。
- 由于我们的员工数量减少了，我们可以同心协力干一番事业。
- 我们的团队正处于一个良好的成长起点，并且可以引入精干的新鲜力量。
- 我们都是对公司忠心耿耿的员工，我们有责任使公司继续发展并且超越竞争对手。

激励他们的主人翁责任感，询问他们的想法并且加以实施

使用积极向上的语言，要关注未来的发展，不要在消极方面踌躇不前。

错误用语：

- 如果你们有任何问题的话可以告诉我。
- 我们不想失去你们。请告诉我们你们的困难，我们会解决。
- 我知道目前有一些困难，有些人因此而离开了。那么我们该怎样才能做得更好呢？

正确用语：

- 为了使公司的工作环境变得更好，你们有什么好的想法？
- 大家都知道我们有一个意见箱，请把你们的想法告诉我们，而且请别忘了在会议上也提出你们的想法，我们很乐于倾听。

- 对于公司的未来，你们有什么设想？

以目标激励他们

- 我们计划继续成长，并尽我们所能回报社会。
- 我们将继续维护我公司的形象。作为一家强大的、利润丰厚的公司，我们注重公德、保持公正。
- 在相互交往中，我们将继续尊重自己，尊重他人。
- 我们将继续前进，寻求新的、激动人心的技术来改变所有人的生活。
- 我们将成长为业内最富创新精神、最成功的企业。

建立清晰的目标

不管目标是什么，要强调你们将作为一个团队一起工作，来共同完成目标。

- 今后 3 年，我们将共同努力把我们的利润翻一番。
- 我们的目标是在 3 个区域里开设新的分支机构，我们将紧密团结、共同努力，你们将由于自己的成功而获得回报。
- 我们的唯一目标就是使成员人数在年底达到新的高度，我们将通过富于进取心和开放性的工作关系来做到这一点。

你们的公司遭遇恶意收购

现在，你们的公司相当于被对手掌握了。面对现实吧，你仍然在此工作，你的团队仍然在此工作。谁知道呢，也许你们甚至会喜欢上新公司。但首要的是说服你的同事和员工，使他们不至于离你而去。使用以下这些完美措辞，再加上一点时间，会有所帮助的。

公布消息

如果你是团队负责人或者经理，你可能需要向员工宣布这一消息。最好能及时宣布以消除谣言和媒体的影响，让员工们知道被收购的事实。要小心仔细，以实事求是和积极正面的态度来组织语言。

● 我刚刚知道，________公司已成为我们的母公司。我并不认为会有特别剧烈的变化，所以我们静观事态的进展吧。

● ________已经完成了交易。按我的理解，这将使工作环境变得更加好起来，这家公司向来在员工待遇方面投入很大。

● 如你们所知，我们现在开始为________工作，我们的业务和良好业绩将一如既往。实际上，唯一发生变化的只是公司的名称和少数最高层的管理者。

小提示

让员工确信你将使他们获得及时、重要的信息，并且详细、确切地告知他们你将如何做到这一点。引起员工焦虑的主要原因之一就是他们感觉自己在任人摆布，定时地更新信息将对他们有极大的帮助。

● 我将在每周一的例会上把最新的变化通知你们。

● 如果你们听到什么传闻，不要相信。马上来找我，我可以告诉你们真相。

● 我将给你们所有人发送电子邮件，定期更新关于公司合并的消息。

● 我将参加每周的经理会议，会议一结束你们就可以到小会议室来找我，我会告诉你们所有的最新进展。

若同事或雇员表示愤怒或关切

● 你们应该静观其变，到目前为止我们也一无所知。

● 这样的变化是职场中的常事，所以，就当帮自己一把，别再忧心忡忡的了，只要耐心等待、静静观察就可以了。

● 这家公司的利润很高，并且有更多的成长机会，所以这可能是一件好事。

● 面对未知的未来确实很困难，但这是一家稳定的公司，我对此事持乐观的态度。

● 变化总是让人感到不安，不管是否必须如此，我们都需要做个深呼吸，放松一下，然后等着看将会发生什么。

处理与人事部门有关的业务

除了要说服其他人公司并没有陷入困境之外，还要说服自己。所以，要询问一些重要的事项并获得可靠的信息。如果是好消息，那太棒了；如果是坏消息，提前知道也比不知道要好。仔细想想自己究竟需要一些什么样的信息，以下这些例子都是你可以问的问题：

● 我的医疗保险计划将会是什么样的？

● 这家公司以往的人员保留率是什么样的？

● 它的内部晋升政策是怎样的？

● 这家公司以往在解雇员工方面的情况如何？

● 这家公司在多大程度上依赖承包商？

● 公司的培训计划如何？

● 这家公司是否有重大的社区活动或者慈善活动计划？公司关于捐赠的政策如何？

记住不要问主观性的问题，人事部的人员不会（也不应该）表达其个人观点。

不要问：

● 你喜欢这家公司吗？

● 你觉得公司值得信任吗？

● 你觉得公司将在什么时候开始对我们发难？

● 你觉得我们在这家公司的职位有保障吗？

● 我确实很喜欢自己的经理，你觉得他会留任吗？

● 这家公司是否会发生突然的、无法预测的变化？

拜会新领导

可以借此机会询问关于前景、时间安排以及政策性的问题，这些都是人事部门人员无法回答的。用事实来充实你的问话，这样可以确保新领导给予清晰的、有益的答复。

- 您接管________公司时，关闭了客户服务部门，将其外包至海外。您对本公司也打算如此吗？
- 公司的具体目标是什么？比如说，打算继续扩张吗？
- 我们这两家公司之间的文化差异有哪些？我们所能期待的是什么？

Part Five

In the Fire of Sabotage and Insubordination

Yes, work is hard enough. But having to address other people's ill will, from undercutting comments to unfulfilled tasks, only makes it harder. Yet, like many other communications in difficult situations, your response can have legal implications. You never know which ones may show up in court or your lawyer may use to get money that belongs to you. So you must remember several points when writing: consider them your defense, your strategy, and, above all, your legal armor should the worst occur:

- **Document everything.** Make sure you e-mail repeating every important communication, and save it for years to come. You never know when the problem will haunt you—even when it seems to be resolved. Talk on the phone? Have a meeting? Then follow up with an e-mail repeating the major points in your discussion.
- **Get witnesses.** Make sure that you have witnesses, particularly when discussing egregious behavior. You may want to mention the person in passing by saying something like: "In our meeting with Joel, you said . . ." Or keep your own records. Regardless, cc'ing someone, whether a boss, lawyer, or senior-level expert, always helps.
- **Use objective language.** Be sure that you use accurate and specific language—with no feelings involved. For example, avoid saying: "You insulted me in front of the group." This would meet a simple denial, as in: "No, I did not." Instead, be clear and say: "At the meeting on the 19th, you said that I was 'too stupid to think straight'" and other insulting lines. If someone is raising his or her voice, try to add an objective quality by saying, for example: "Several customers asked Carl what the commotion was all about."
- **Be clear about what you want.** The reason you send a message about an

inappropriate or counterproductive interaction is simply to inspire a response. But what should that response consist of? Do you want them to stop engaging in a certain behavior? Leave a project? Get fired? Or do you want them to pay a bill . . . with interest? Be clear about what you want in your own mind—then state it on the page. Otherwise, you're just letting off steam.

- **Never pose a threat you don't mean.** Very often, if you're angry or tired of dealing with a difficult situation (yet again), you might be tempted to threaten to call an attorney, report them to an association or consumer agency, or take some other action. Be sure not to threaten something you don't mean though; you may want to make them shiver with fear, but they might call their attorney instead.

A Constant Air of Passive-Aggressive Whining Undermines Team Morale and Energy

Passive-aggressive behavior, especially en masse, can be deadly. You don't know what to expect, how to strategize, or whom to trust. So your main mission is to take control, making tasks, professional relationships, and even behavior as clear and indisputable as possible.

When Passive-Aggressive Colleagues Sabotage You on a Project

Focus on the project—rather than on yourself—even when you think the passive-aggressive behavior is personal.

First: State the negative actions using objective and measurable language:

- We agreed that you would_____ by Friday. Yet you didn't complete that task, nor did you notify me or anyone else on the team that you wouldn't.
- On the telephone at 9 a.m., you said that you would have _____ ready. When I arrived, though, you were unprepared.
- You told me that you would _____ for four hours a day. Yet the records indicate that you did not take these steps even once.
- In our project plan, you were supposed to _____ by _____. Yet now you claim you haven't even started on that task.

Then: Show how that affected the team:

●As a result, we will not be able to ______, as planned. This will create cash flow problems, as we cannot bill until you have completed these steps.

●I was unable to work with our client in a fast and effective manner. As a result, the customer was dissatisfied, as you know from her e-mail to the boss.

●We do not ________, as we agreed in our game plan. This sets us back by weeks, possibly months.

●Three of us will have to pitch in to stay on track.

Next: Discuss what you expect from the team:

●You must complete ______ plus ______ to make up for the delay. We will follow up on your progress in our Tuesday meetings.

●You must send the customer an apology note and offer to make up for the problem somehow. Please cc me and the boss on this.

●You must provide ____ by _____.

●You must get started immediately and send all of us on the team a running record.

When Colleagues' Gossip Undermines Your Reputation in the Office

Confront them directly, and state that you want that behavior to stop:

●I understand that you have plenty to say about the state of my personal life. This kind of attack is unprofessional, and you need to stop.

●According to several people in the office, you said that _____. This makes you look bad—as well as me—and you need to stop.

●Keep your comments about my personal life to yourself.

●If you have comments on my work style, say them to me.

Sometimes, passive-aggressive colleagues attempt to undermine your power by telling you the negative comments other people have told them about you. This is hurtful, unprofessional, and inappropriate, so tell them to stop:

●Please stop telling me that ____ doesn't like the way I dress. It doesn't have anything to do with work.

●You seem to be getting a lot of insights about what people think of me personally. This leads me to think you are gossiping about me—this is unprofessional, and you should stop.

- I really don't care what _____ or anyone else thinks about my _____, so don't bother to tell me.

When getting control of employees who undermine your authority through passive-aggressive behavior:

- Once we decide that _____, it's not negotiable or up for discussion.
- If you have issues about my management style, schedule a meeting, and we'll discuss them.
- I understand that many of you have had doubts about the project. It's counterproductive to discuss them among yourselves; we should have a meeting to discuss them together.
- If you have any questions about the project, bring them directly to me or one of the team leaders—we can give you an accurate response.

Follow the phrase with an objective example of how they undermined your authority.

When Addressing a Group of Employees Who Are Stuck in Whine Mode

- From now on, let's discuss what can happen, not what didn't.
- Let's write all your complaints in one column of the flip chart page and the solutions in the other.
- Why not break into groups and draw up a plan for how you will solve these problems?
- What do all of you think is a good approach?

If you don't get a spoken response, stop the meeting and suggest they write a few ideas down and then report in.

Associates Try to Steal Your Project

Maybe your associates think they're better qualified for the work. More entitled. Or that a loophole in a contract allows them to take it from you. No matter—if the project is yours and you worked hard on it, work equally hard to keep it with these perfect phrases.

When You Realize Someone Is Trying to Steal Your Project

State how you know what the person is up to and provide evidence that the project is yours. The order doesn't matter—just be sure that you are concrete and support your points:

- _____ told me that you were planning to _____ in the project. Our contract specifies that my company is responsible for this aspect of the job, as you can see in this paragraph: (***quote paragraph***).
- I recently learned that you were _____. In my meeting on December 6, the client asked me to be responsible for this task, and we have begun that project already. I have e-mails which support this fact. I can send them if you like.
- According to our agreement, we are responsible for _____ through the summer of 2010. If you would like to add your employees to the project, contact me directly and we'll discuss whether we have a need.
- As we agreed in April 2007, you are a subcontractor to us. As a result, you cannot initiate any actions on this project without first consulting with us.

Alert the Client or Project Manager

Be friendly and matter-of-fact. You don't want to embroil your client in an angry interaction between you and the other party.

- Just to let you know, we have already begun to _____, as you requested on June 14. We just learned that _____ is undertaking similar steps; thought you'd like to know before we duplicate efforts.
- I spoke with ___ yesterday. Apparently, ___ is planning to _____. We already agreed to undertake that aspect of the project and have experts in place and will continue moving forward.
- As you know, we have a project plan in place and have already initiated the first two phases. ______ may have a plan of their own; switching gears partway into the project will be time consuming and expensive.

When helpful, get the client to support your side of the situation:

- As we discussed in the team meeting, you want us to _____ by _____. If this is not the case, let me know.
- According to our contract, my team is responsible for _____. ______ has told us

that it is planning to take over this task. Could you clarify so we can continue moving ahead?

● Some questions have been coming up about who is responsible for _____. Could you please confirm?

Alert Your Colleagues or Staff to the Situation

● As you know, we have been providing ____ with _____ services for two years. This is in our contract. If you see that anyone is taking over these tasks, please let me know.

● We have been working as the lead on the _____ project, which we won through a competitive bid in 2003. Our contract is good for another two years. Should you receive instruction from anyone else, please notify me at once.

● According to an e-mail I received recently, _____ is planning to engage in the _____ that we have been working on. Yet _____ is not authorized to do so. If anything changes, please let me know.

Your Company or Business Partners Are Lying to the Client About the Scope of Work So They Get More Business

No question—not everyone is cut out to be a whistle-blower, especially when alerting a client about the client's own company. But you may not have to take such drastic steps. Just letting your colleagues know they're doing the wrong thing may be enough to stop them. Here are some perfect phrases that can help, without getting you in hot water.

When Providing Feedback About a Proposal

● This looks good, except for line 1. We've never needed that much time to _____. Why don't we cut down by two days?

● We can cut the time for our services in half if we eliminate ____ and ____. This won't affect the outcome, and the client will be happy with the rate.

● In our previous proposals, we only needed _____ amount of time for the _____. Unless there's a good reason, let's provide our standard arrangement.

- I think this proposal is really overpriced. We should aim for ____. That's only fair for the client.

When Discussing a Project at a Meeting

- I think we need to discuss the realistic costs under the "scope of work" section.
- Guys, we do really great work, but I'm concerned that we're overcharging the client.
- I understand that we're adding "padding" just in case. How about if we give them a price range and try to stay low?
- This proposal doesn't seem quite fair, as our rates have not gone up; yet this client would pay 25 percent more than everyone else.

When Determining How to Bill the Client That Week

Be straightforward, and focus your comments on individual expenses. Be sure to discuss individual dates and times. The specifics will depend on your situation, obviously, but may sound like this:

- We charged them for two business lunches on May 10 and 21. I attended both lunches, but we didn't discuss the client once.
- We only spent two hours, from 3:00 to 5:00, on the project on January 10.
- Let me know if you want me to review my notes, but I'm certain that Lonny didn't attend the May 1 debrief, so we can't bill them for his time.
- I invited our employees to meet with the client as a friendly gesture on December 30, but not as a work session. So we shouldn't bill them.

Service Providers Don't Supply What They Promised

Nowhere else is documentation as helpful as here. You must document every agreement, what they did or didn't provide, and evidence that this occurred. Write the occurrences down as they happen; then when e-mailing or talking to the provider, you should use your records as evidence to support your point.

When Pointing Out the Problem

●In my contract, you stated that you would provide____. I never received this service.

●You stated that you would provide ____ on ____. I received the service two days late, and it has been interrupted three times since.

●In my agreement, you said a ___ and ____ would be assigned to help me. Yet I have not heard from any of them.

●You said that___, who is in charge of my account, would help me ____ and ____. Yet _____ denies that these are his responsibilities.

When the Problem Persists

●When I signed on for the service, I agreed to pay $____ for the following: ____. I only received these services: (***list, with the dates you received them***) although you billed me for the complete package.

●As I stated in my e-mail of May 14, I still have not received ____. Also the ___ that you provided has the following problems: ____. I contacted ____ about this several times the week of May 1 but have not seen an improvement.

●Since August 14, when I first signed on for your service, I have encountered the following problems: ____. I have documented each of these in detail and can send my notes if you like.

When You Get What You Requested but the Product or Service Is Bad

●The ____ that you sent me has the following problems: ____.

●While your employees have provided the services in your agreement, they did not respond to my calls on ___ and ____ and did not fix the ___ that was not working correctly from ___ to ___.

●I have consistently had problems with the services that you provide, particularly with the ___ and the ___. I have e-mailed you about these problems. I can send copies if you like.

●You did not provide the ___ or the ____, as stated in my contract. Further, the ____ had the following problems: _____. I outlined these in numerous e-mails as well as telephone conversations, all of which I have documented.

You Get Charged for Services You Didn't Want

- I have been receiving your _____ since ____ although I never requested it. Although I asked you to discontinue the service, you continue to provide it.
- Please stop sending me the _____. I never asked to receive it and do not intend to pay my bill.
- I just realized that you added ____ to my normal bill. You never informed us that we would have to pay extra for this service. Please discontinue the service and strike the expense from my monthly bill.
- My associate informed me that you have been billing us for _____ under the _____. Yet we never received this service, nor do we want it.

Quick tip

In some cases, you may want compensation for poor service. If so, how do you know what to request? And when to request it? My advice—let them make the move. Here's why: you may be asking for less than they're willing to give. In that case, you're stuck. If they offer less than you want, you can always demand more.

Here are a few perfect phrases when demanding compensation. *And remember*: Be fair and be tough!

- Please tell me how you will compensate me for these problems.
- What do you plan to do about these problems in the future?
- How will you make up the difference to me?
- I derailed my project goals because of these problems. How do you plan to address this?
- These problems have been costly: I can send you a breakdown of expenses I've incurred as a result. You need to compensate me for the difference.

There's a Sudden Exodus of Employees to Your Competitor

And they're . . . off. Employees, who loved you and your firm, run off to the competitor. How do you stop more from leaving? And how do you manage without them? And . . . how do you manage morale issues with the ones who are left? Perfect phrases are in order here. But first check your own morale, and remember, every chaotic event offers a chance to move ahead.

Create a Sense of Belonging to the Team

People are leaving, and everyone knows it. Rather than be in denial, why not discuss the event—even leverage it—to create a team that's stronger than before. Here are some ways to do that:

- Well, some folks have left, and we miss them. But this is a great chance to set a newer and stronger direction for all of us.
- Since we're a smaller staff now, we can really pull together and make things happen.
- We're in a great position to grow as a team and bring in new people who are sharp and energetic.
- We're the die-hard loyalists, and it's up to us to make sure our company continues to grow, and grow beyond the competitors.

Get Them to Take Ownership: Ask Their Opinions and Follow Through

Rely on positive language, and focus on what's ahead. Avoid dwelling on the negatives.

Don't

- If you have any problems, let me know.
- We don't want to lose you, so let us know what bothers you and we'll see what we can do.
- I know things have been tough around here and that's why people are leaving. So what can we do to become better than we are?

Do

- What are some ideas you have for making the company an even better place to work?
- As you know, we have a suggestion box. Please let us know your thoughts,

and be sure to raise your ideas at meetings, too. We're open to hearing them.

- What would you like to see as the future of our company?

Infuse Them with a Sense of Purpose

- We plan to continue growing and giving back to the community as we do.
- As always, we want to maintain our reputation as a strong, profitable company that is ethical and fair.
- We'll continue treating ourselves and others with respect in all our interactions.
- We plan to forge ahead, finding new and exciting technologies that improve the lives of everyone.
- We plan to grow into the most innovative and successful company in our region.

Create Clear Goals and Objectives

Whatever the goals and objectives, underscore that you will achieve them by working as a team:

- We'll work together to double our profits within the next three years.
- Our objective is to open branch locations in the three districts. We'll work closely together and reward you for your success.
- Our single goal is to build our membership to record highs by the end of the year. We can do this through an aggressive and open working relationship.

Your Company Gets Bought Out in a Hostile Situation

So now your company is at the hands of what's tantamount to the enemy. But face it—you're still there. Your team's still there. And who knows, maybe you'll even like the new company. But the trick is to convince your coworkers and employees so they don't abandon you. These perfect phrases, and a little time, will help.

When Breaking the News

If you're a team leader or a manager, you may need to break the news to your employees. Better get there quickly, too, and beat the rumor mill and the media. Let them know about the buyout or takeover, being careful to frame it in the most realistic and positive sense.

- I just learned that _____ is now our parent company. I'm not expecting any elaborate changes, so let's keep focusing on what's ahead.
- ______ has just closed the deal. As I understand it, this might make the workplace better. The company has a history of investing heavily in its employees.
- Just so you know, we're now working for _____. Our mission and the great services will remain the same. In fact, it's possible the only thing that will change is our name and some of the senior-most managers.

Quick tip

Let employees feel confident that you'll keep them in the information loop. Be specific—let them know exactly how you'll do this. Remember, one of the major sources of anxiety for employees is feeling out of control. Regular updates can help them immeasurably:

- I'll update you about changes in our regular Monday meeting.
- If you hear gossip, don't believe it. Come to me immediately, and I'll tell you what's true and what isn't.
- I'll e-mail all of you regular updates about the merger as news comes in.
- I'll be attending the weekly manager's meeting. So plan to meet with me immediately after in the small conference room. I'll fill you in about any changes.

When Coworkers and Employees Express Anger or Concern

- You need to wait until you see what changes happen. So far, we have no idea.
- Changes like these are just part of business life. So do yourself a favor and don't worry about it. Just wait and see.
- This company is highly profitable and has more opportunities for growth. So this may be a good thing.
- It's hard to know what's ahead. But it's a solid company, and I'm optimistic.

- Change can feel hard, regardless of whether or not it's merited by reality. I think we all need to breathe deeply, relax, and wait to see what's ahead.

When Addressing Issues with HR Representatives

Aside from convincing others the company isn't going to the dark side, you may need to convince yourself. So ask the right questions and get concrete information. If the news is good—great! If the news is bad—you're still better off knowing it. Think hard, though, about what you really need to know. Here are some examples of questions you might ask:

- What can I expect from my health insurance plan?
- What is the company's retention history?
- What is its policy about promoting from within?
- What is its history regarding layoffs?
- How heavily does the company rely on contractors?
- What are its training programs like?
- Does the company have strong community and charitable programs? What are the company's policies regarding giving?

Remember, do not ask subjective questions. It's unlikely the HR representative will (or should) express his or her perspective from a personal point of view.

Don't Ask

- Do you like this company?
- Do you think it's trustworthy?
- When do you think it will start making life hard for us?
- So you think we have job security with this company?
- I really love my manager. Think he'll be on his way out?
- Is it the type of company that makes sudden, unpredictable changes?

When Meeting New Leadership

This is your chance to ask questions about vision, timing, and policy issues the HR representative couldn't address. Come fueled with facts that help frame your question and enable the new leaders to give you clear and helpful answers.

●When you took over ____ Company, you closed the customer care unit and outsourced it abroad. Do you have plans to do this here?

●What are your goals for the company in concrete terms? For example, do you plan to continue expanding?

●What are some of the culture differences between our two companies, and what can we expect?

第六章

应对压力

工期完不成、完工日期不明朗或者遥遥无期，这些都是职业生活的一部分内容。对此，有些人能应付过来，而多数人则不能。无论如何，这需要充沛的精力和清醒的头脑，而你发出的信息必须能够反映并且激发这些要素。这意味着，你必须摒弃拖沓冗长的句子、令人厌烦的词语以及厚重、乏味的段落。这些都意味着“迟缓”，将被听众忽视。因而，要让你的话语节奏明快、激情澎湃，激励人们不断前进，前进，再前进。以下是一些要点。

● **使用短句。**这可以使听众感受到迫切性、使命感和重要性。设想一下，如果你看见浓烟正从办公室的窗口飘出，你会采用以下哪种讲话方式？

▲ 如果你们向七楼窗外看，也就是自助餐厅的方位，会看到大量浓密的白色烟雾。我猜想那里是发生了火灾，但不知道为什么没有响警报。最好我们全部撤离现场吧！

▲ 瞧，七楼着火了！窗子正在冒烟！就在自助餐厅里。警报怎么没响？快走，我们赶紧撤离！

你自然会选择第二种方式。所以，在讲述时间紧迫的事情时，不要慢条斯理地，否则听众也会行动迟缓。

● **避免使用专业术语。**这不是使用专业术语的时候，它们只会产生一种迟缓的感觉。相反，为了使你的语言更有力量，要使用犀利的动词、简短精练的词组以及常用的词汇。简言之，这种情况下请使用日常生活用语。

● **要直接、确切地告诉听众应该做些什么。**不要使用建议或引导的口吻，而是以命令的语气告诉对方要这样做。注意这两种表达方式的区别。

▲ 你按时把相关材料交给我，这是很重要的。最晚要在今天下班之前，这样我才能按时把它们交给查理。

▲ 下午 5 点之前把这些交给我，我审阅后交给查理。

● **注意标题行。**如果使用电子邮件的话，一定要使标题行富于激情，每一个词语都要极富表现力，并且显示出该信息的紧迫性。

以下将提供更多的方法和大量的完美措辞。

项目时间紧迫

你的要求很明确——让对方放下手头的任何事情，立刻行动起来。所以，你的话要快速、清晰、简洁。在这种情况下最好是电话和邮件双管齐下，因为你也不知道哪一种方式更快一些。如果你确实通过电话先与对方联系上了，随后也要发一封电子邮件，写明任务和期限，以免混淆。

电子邮件标题行

要简短，只用一个有震撼力的词语即可。

错误写法：

● 今天上交 XYZ 报表

● 今日项目要求

● IT 部门急需的报告

● 昨天就该提交预算了

正确写法：

● 马上提交行程表!

● 下午两点项目必须完成

● 紧急期限

- 急需提交预算

运用幽默和讽刺可以使标题行富有激情。程度的把握取决于你所在的公司、收信人以及事情的严重程度。以下是一些例句。

严肃且有效

- 马上提交行程表!

幽默且有效

- 今天交表，否则不许来上班!
- 飞机还等着呢!

严肃且有效

- 马上提交预算!

幽默且有效

- 下午3点交表，否则别想要钱!
- 想要钱，最好快点!
- 预算银行正在关门!

小提示

尽量使用日常用语，即使对名称也是如此。XX预算表的名称是B08-262（为什么这么称呼只有你们公司知道），如果将邮件标题写为“该交B08-262了”，就会混入大量带有类似标题的邮件之中，毫不起眼，无法引起收件人的注意。不如使用日常用语“马上提交预算表”，然后在邮件正文中详述该表格即可。

可能的话，给收件人一点告诫。但是，必须要真诚，不能捏造——尽管这样做很吸引人。

- 只剩两个培训名额了!
- 今天提交预算，否则就没有经费。
- 医疗计划选择下午5点结束。

电子邮件正文

详述标题栏中提到的相关内容，但是请注意，仍然要避免拖沓冗长的句子以及喋喋不休的介绍。所以，不要使用类似以下的开场白。

错误写法：

- 今天早些时候与项目负责人一起开会时，我了解到我们的完成日期已经由原定的周五紧急提前到今天下午。
- 我想要提醒你们一下，今天下午4点前把物资采购表交给我，否则的话你们就得等到2月份才能进行采购。
- 我刚听到一位客户说了关于新产品的事。他说，根据合同我们应该在5月1日提交________，现在已经延误两周了。如果我们不马上送货的话，他就要诉诸法律了。我检查了与他之间的合同，确实如他所说。

正确写法：

- 重要提示：原定周五的期限紧急提前到今天下午，所有的东西都必须在下午4点前交给我。
- 如果下午4点前不上交物资采购表，就只能等到2月再进行采购。
- 今天必须给客户发送一份新的________否则他将诉诸法律。注意：我们已经延误了，他有足够的理由这样做。

电话用语

像写邮件一样，要直奔主题，省去那些友好的寒暄和客套，诸如“您有时间吗”。当然，具体怎么说取决于你的实际情况，不过大致可以这样说：

- 我们手上有个很紧迫的任务。
- 麦凯恩公司的最后期限迫在眉睫了，你们必须在下午4点之前把所有东西都交给我。
- 查理刚来过电话，让我们必须在下午3点前向财务部提交预算，否则项目就要泡汤了。
- 如果你们想报销这次差旅费，就必须在午饭前把费用明细交给贝丝。否则，直到 2 月份你们都别想得到一分钱。

突发问题导致期限紧迫

当问题突然出现时，你必须提醒大家，但是不要引起他们的慌乱、愤怒或者其他的负面情绪。相反，应该把他们的注意力集中到解决方案上。

若影响到客户

要尽快向客户解释一下发生了什么事以及对其有何影响，即使客户已经获悉此事，也要如此办理。

- ________刚刚提醒我们________和________发生故障停机了。我们必须马上进行修复，否则的话将会发生……
- 我们配置在________办公室里的________发生了故障。马上与承包商联系，我这就赶到客户那去。
- ________死机了，请马上把它修好，我会和客户保持联系。
- 我们上周承诺给客户的________还没有准备好，必须马上完成。

要使用强有力的有刺激性的动词，不要使用不瘟不火的词语。

不可用	可用
告诉	警告
说	宣布
不工作	中止 / 死机 / 停机

发现安全事故

告诉大家发生了什么以及他们应该如何应对。不要危言耸听，也不要喋喋不休地讲他们必须马上行动的原因。

- 重要公告：系统发现……大楼中的所有人都将受到影响。
- 在________发现了安全隐患，必须马上关闭整座大楼。

● 楼内发现三个未佩带安全标识的外来者，请通知相关人员进行检查（最后发现他们的地点是接待室）。

● 我们这层楼的防盗门被撬开了，我刚刚通知了保安，你们最好也检查一下自己的门。

团队成员犯了巨大（而且愚蠢）的错误

与当事人谈话

● 你为客户开发的________死机了，必须马上把它修好，否则的话将影响到……

● 你错把________发给了客户，马上给他更换正确的________并且给他的经理发一份跟踪回访记录。

● 我们安排你去做________而你忽视了这一点。现在，……已经……了，你必须马上采取以下措施：……

小提示

当你向他人求助时，有时需要说明该错误是谁的责任，有时则需谨慎，不要提及任何人的名字。这取决于几个因素：情况的发展变化、对方对结果产生的影响力大小以及求助对象对相关任务了解多少。

● XX 忘记保存文件了，我们无法查到重要的客户信息。你能帮我们查一下吗？

● 周五 XX 没有与他的客户定好时间，所以客户今天并未打算会见我们，请立即与他们联系一下。

● XX 忘记送交________了，你能替他送去吗？因为他正在开会。

● 电脑中的________工作异常，请你看看有没有办法。很紧急！

小提示

一定要表达清楚、准确。无论你是处在危机之中也好、在解决问题也好，或者是在赶工期也好，都要让听众清楚地知道发生了什么、该做些什么以及何时做。顺便说一下，不要提前太早，这样会对你不利，因为人们有可能会忘掉。如果确实是提前通知的话，一定要在期限迫近时再补充提醒一次。

错误用语：

- 尽快（到底什么时候？）
- 一旦你方便的话，就……（永远不会有方便的时候）
- 什么时候能做你就什么时候做。（几乎永远都不会做）

正确用语：

- 马上。
- 1 小时之内。
- 今天 5 点之前。

限期紧张源于竞争对手威胁要抢先发布新产品或者抢先开展新业务

实际上，宣布这样的限期通知是最容易的。这种情况为你提供了外部力量推动员工行动起来，使其充满力量和斗志，并且营造了一种良好的、竞技性的工作氛围。这还能告诉你竞争何时能见分晓。以下完美措辞有助于你的起跑。

刚获知此消息时

一般来说，你应该按以下结构来组织语言。

你所听到的……为了与之竞争必须做到的……

- 我们刚刚听说……让我们争取在下周启动________。
- ________将于今年夏初推出他们的新款……我们必须加紧努力，并且争取在________时推出自己的产品。
- ________正打算进入________领域，我们最好马上加强在该领域的宣传力度，得马上与公关部门联系一下。
- 刚刚获知，________将要……与广告部门联系一下，我们需要一场攻势强劲的宣传。

以下是几个详细的示例：

- 刚刚获知马歇尔公司将于今夏在波士顿开一家新店，我们最好加紧完成与地产商之间的协议，确保我们能在今春开业。
- 理查德－戴维斯投资公司将于两周内启动他们的新项目，通知公关部门抢先发布一些消息，这样我们就能立刻引起轰动。
- 刚刚获悉全技术公司正在计划推出最新版本的软件，我们的软件准备好发布了吗？看看研发部门能否加快速度。

当你的团队行动迟缓

可以使用“如果我们不能……那么将会……”的句式。

如果我们不能……那么将会……

- 如果我们不能在 5 月完成……那么……将首先上市。
- 如果我们不能尽快找到办公地点，那么……将进入我们的市场。
- 如果我们不能抓紧完成产品的开发，就来不及让它们上架了。
- 如果我们不采取攻势宣传，就会被他们的广告淹没了！

或者可以把相关的利益摆在前面，比如“为了能够……我们必须……”。

为了能够……，我们必须……

- 为了能够吸引媒体的注意，我们必须抢先发布该产品。
- 为了能促使人们签约，我们必须在下月发起一场挨家挨户上门的宣传活动。
- 为了能使大家与我们签约，我们必须在假期来临之前游说购物中心。

采用哪一种说法更有利取决于你所要讲的内容。

你搞砸了一个项目，必须对客户做出解释

火烧眉毛时就不要讲究礼仪了。你搞砸了一个项目，受此影响最大的就是你的客户。所以，要表现出关切，而不要惊慌失措；要表示歉意，而不要卑躬屈膝；要行动迅速，不要让局面陷入混乱。啊！然后该怎么办呢？跟踪回访，确保客户原谅了你，并且愿意继续合作。

通知客户

这确实需要一些策略。如果问题相对容易解决，就讲一下你的必要措施以及相关理由。

- 我们需要重装________，以使您的……重新工作起来。
- 由于原件已经烧毁了，我们需要更换________。这只需占用您 1 个小时的时间。
- 我们需要……这项工作很简单。您的________将重起，并且在 1 个小时之内开始工作。

如果需要花费时间解决问题，那就介绍一下情况以及你的处理方式。

- ……不可靠，脱离了原位，所以，我们需要……
- 由于广告复印件上有几处拼写错误，我们不得不重新设计并且重新打印，这需要额外的两周时间。
- 我们发现________的尺寸不正确，需要重新建造一个。

可能的话，强调你们的认真维修可以带来的好处。

- 这将确保……
- 由此带来的结果是________的性能会比事故前还要好。
- 在此过程中，我们将检查任何的……
- 我们还将仔细检查________，这有利于你们将来……
- 在此过程中我们将记录所有的________，并且告知你们，这将有助于你们……

避免使用过分消极的语言，情况已经很糟了，别再雪上加霜。

错误用语：

- 不幸的是，在我们修好之前，你们不能……了。
- 我们无法……
- 现在的这台设备不能使用了。
- 你在……之前无法开始。

正确用语：

- 一旦我们维修完毕，你们就能……了。
- 我们仍然需要……
- 我们将给你们更换新的________。
- 在________时候你就可以开始了。

提议额外的补偿

应该在首次与对方联系时就提及此内容，并且在跟踪回访时还要再次提到。通常可以采用如下说法：

- 为了补偿本次延期，我们将……
- 当然，我们的________是免费的。
- 我们将在您的合同中加入额外的……
- 除……之外，我们将送给您一个________以表达我们的歉意。
- ________和________的正常价格是________美元，但我们将只收取您________美元，这完全是成本价。

对出了问题的项目进行跟踪回访

不要再提及所出现的问题，也不必再次道歉。相反，要强调一下你已经按照承诺向他们提供了所需的服务或产品。

- 根据________中的承诺，我送来了……
- 请注意，我们给您提供的________和________都是免费的。
- 在 4 月份，我们承诺将合同免费延长 1 个月，所以我们将免费继续为您服务。

- 您可以在发票的第 5 行看到，我们给您打了________（百分比）的折扣。

由于法律或其他方面的新规定，你必须改变你的员工规则、文件或者流程

对于员工而言，遵守现有的规章制度已经很难了，违规事件难以避免，甚至还可能遭遇诉讼，所以，更别说有新的规章、条例、政策出台了。此时，你必须迅速采取管理措施来应对。为何如此之难呢？原因之一是，人们在遵守现有规则时形成了惯性，他们习惯于按旧有的方式来工作。现在，突然要求他们做出改变则需要付出额外的思考和精力，并且会有一定的滞后，所以，你需要促使他们集中注意力。同时，面对不同的变化，还需要考虑士气问题。超负荷工作的员工面对变化可能会缺乏耐心，并且可能会有挫折感。

用以下完美措辞激励员工，促使其集中精力并且保持高昂的士气。

宣布新规则

让员工们知道是谁引发了这些变化，尤其是当你们公司与此无关时。

- ________部在今年秋季制定了这些新条例。
- 由于……发生的变化，我们必须调整关于……的政策。
- ________发布了新规定，我们必须遵守。我把复印件发下来供你们阅读。
- 根据________，从本月 1 日起，所有关于________的要求都已改变。从现在起，你们必须做以下事情……

表示关注

讲明你将如何支持他们，要讲得详细、具体，即使还没有定好确切的时间也要讲一下具体内容。

- 我们将举办研究班，教会你们如何应对新规则，虽然现在还不知道具体时间，但是会很快通知你们。

● 公司已经制定了一本手册来回答你们的问题。

● 你们可以随时（在家里也可以）参加一个在线培训课程。

再三承诺他们将会获得帮助，要具体提供联系人的姓名、电子邮箱、电话号码，必要时给出具体的时间。

● 你们有问题的话可以找人事部的________，从上午8点到下午5点的任何时间都可以，他的分机号码是________

● 问询台已经完全准备好了，可以回答你们的疑问，你们可以在工作日的任何时间给那里的人打电话或者发电子邮件咨询。

● 如果你们对将要做的事感到迷惑的话，请给我发邮件或者直接来找我，只要我办公室的门开着，就尽管进来。

应对愤怒或者其他阻力。

● 我知道这看起来有点困难，但你们很快就会习惯的。

● 很快就会习惯了。

● 放松点，以前的规则刚刚引入时每个人都觉得很复杂，但现在看来都很简单，这次也一样。

对新规则拿不准时该如何向他人询问。

● 如果发生了……该怎么做?

● 这将对……的情况有何种影响?

● 他们为什么要改变现行的程序？

● 如果我对法律方面的影响不清楚，该去找谁询问?

● 公司将提供什么样的培训?

● 公司全体都要执行这一新政策吗? 还是只有我们部门执行?

● 我们怎么知道自己做错了?

询问以下问题来确认如何应对客户的顾虑。

● 我们的客户知道这些变化吗?

● 如果客户问起为什么改变程序，该如何回答?

● 如果客户对程序改变有疑问的话，我们应该请他们找谁询问?

● 如果客户坚持要求按以往程序执行的话，该怎么办?

● 有这方面的宣传材料可以发给客户吗?

Part Six

Pressure Cookers

Deadlines missed, looming, and unexpected are simply a part of business life. Some people thrive on them; most people don't. Regardless, they require energy and clear thinking, and your messages must reflect and inspire this. That means you must throw away long, dragging sentences, tired phrases, and thick, boring paragraphs that reflect a certain slowness that the recipient will ignore. Instead, keep your message fast and exciting, inspiring people to move, move, move. Here are some tips about how:

● **Use short sentences.** These give the recipient a sense of speed, mission, and importance. Pretend, for a minute, that you see smoke pouring out of a window in your office. Which would you be more inclined to say:

▲ If you look out the window of the seventh floor, you know, where the cafeteria is located, you'll notice thick, white smoke and lots of it. My assumption is that there's a fire there. I'm not certain about why the alarm hasn't sounded, but it would be preferable if we all got out.

▲ Look! Fire on the seventh floor. Smoke's pouring out the window. Right where the cafeteria is. Why isn't the alarm sounding? Come on; we better get out.

Naturally, you'd say the second option. So don't articulate urgent or timely matters as if you had all day. The recipient will act in kind.

● **Avoid dense language.** This is not the time to use industry language or, worse, jargon. They simply create a slow feel. Instead, energize your message with sharp verbs, short, tight phrases, and accessible words. In short, if you wouldn't use these words in daily conversation, then you shouldn't use them here.

● **Be direct.** Tell your recipients exactly what they need to do. Don't be suggestive or leading. Get to the point. Notice the difference:

▲ It's really important that you get the content to me in a timely fashion—end of day at the latest. This will enable me to get it to Charlie on time.

▲ Get the content to me by 5:00. I'll review it and send it to Charlie.

● Watch those subject lines. If you're sending e-mails, make sure you keep the subject lines peppy. Every word must be energy-charged and reflect that the message within is timely.

More ideas and plenty of perfect phrases wait ahead.

Tight Deadline for a Project

What you want is clear—get the recipient to take an action and drop everything else that he or she is doing. So, yes, keep it fast, clear, and clean. In these situations, it's best to call and e-mail. You never know which will reach the person soonest. If you do connect by phone first, send a follow-up e-mail, including tasks and timing, to avoid any confusion.

Subject Line on an E-Mail

Make it fast—a few explosive words at most.

Don't

● The XYZ form due today

● Project requirement for today

● Implementation plan needed by IT

● Budget deadline was yesterday

Do

● Send travel form now!

● Project deadline 2:00

● Slam deadline on plan!

● Need budget

You can use humor or irony to give your subject line some pizzazz. How far you go obviously depends on your company, the person receiving the e-mail, and the seriousness of the matter. Here are a few examples.

Serious and Effective

- Send travel form now!

Humorous and Effective

- Today: Send form or stay home
- The plane isn't leaving

Serious and Effective

- Need budget now!

Humorous and Effective

- Send it or lose it by 3:00
- Need money? Better hurry!
- Budget bank is closing!

Quick tip

If you have a choice, use the most relaxed language—even with names. Say your budget form is titled B08-262 for reasons only your company knows. Rather than say "B08-262 Due," which will get lost in the typical sea of subject lines wavering in everyone's box, use plain language: "Budget form due now!" Then you can use the form in the body of the text.

When possible, give the recipients a caveat. You must be honest—don't invent, even though it's tempting:

- Two spaces left for training!
- Send budget today or no funding
- Health plan options close at 5:00

Body of an E-mail

Elaborate on the message in your subject line. But remember, you still don't have the luxury of using long, drawn-out sentences or chatty introductions. So avoid openers like these.

Don't

- At my meeting with the project lead earlier today, I learned that our deadline, originally scheduled for Friday, has been bumped up to this afternoon.

- I wanted to remind you that you need to get me the acquisition form by 4:00 today or you will not be able to make purchases until February.
- I heard from a client about the new product. He says that our contract states we would send ___ by May 1—two weeks ago. Unless we send it immediately, he will contact his lawyer. I checked his contract, and he does, indeed, have a case.

Do

- Important: our Friday deadline is now this afternoon. Get me everything by 4:00!
- You cannot make purchases until February if you don't send the acquisition form by 4:00 today.
- We must get the client a new ___ today, or he will contact his lawyer. Note: we're late, and he does have a case.

What to Say in a Phone Call

As in an e-mail, don't warm up with a friendly hello or a sentence like "You gotta minute?" Instead, get right to the point. The specifics depend on your situation, of course, but would sound something like this:

- We have an urgent deadline on our hands.
- The deadline for the McCain client is bumped. You must get me everything by 4:00.
- Charlie just called. We have to get Accounting our budget by 3:00, or the project is off.
- If you want to be reimbursed for the trip, get Beth your expenses before lunch. If not, you won't see a dime until February.

Sudden Deadline Because of Unexpected Problems

When problems pop up, you must alert people without causing them to panic, get angry, or have other strong negative reactions. Instead, get them to take action by focusing on a solution.

When the Client Will Be Affected

Quickly explain what happened and how the client will be affected even if the recipient knows this:

- _____ just alerted us to the fact that ___ and ___ aren't working. We need to repair this immediately, or _____ could occur.
- The _____ that we put in _____'s office has collapsed. Contact the contractor—I'll head to the client's right now.
- The _____ broke. Please fix this right away, and I'll follow up with the client.
- The ___ we promised the client last week still isn't ready. We must get on this right away.

Use strong, excited verbs, not weak ones:

Replace	With
told	alert
said	announced
isn't working	broke/died/stopped

When You Detect a Security Breach

Tell people what happened and what they should do. Don't speculate about the grim possibilities or dwell on the reasons why they must act quickly.

- Important: the system detected ______. This could affect everyone in our building.
- Security breach detected on ______. Shut down the building immediately.
- Three visitors without security tags were spotted in our building. Send officers to investigate, please. Last seen in lobby.
- The security door was propped open on my floor. I just called security—better check your doors.

When Someone on Your Team Made a Big(and Stupid) Mistake

When Speaking to the Person

- The _____ that you developed for the client stopped working. You must correct this immediately; or the ___ and ___ will be affected.

● You accidentally gave the client ______. Get him the correct ___ right away, and send a follow-up notice to his manager.

● We agreed that you would _____. Yet you neglected to do this, and now the _____ is _____. You need to take these steps immediately: ________.

Quick tip

When contacting someone else for support, you may want to discuss who was responsible for the mistake, or you may want to be discreet and not name anyone. This depends on several factors: the dynamics of the situation, how large a role that person played in the outcome, and how much the recipient knows about the task involved.

● _______ neglected to save the files, and we can't locate important client information. Could you see what you can find?

● On Friday, ______ didn't contact her clients about the schedule, so they don't expect us today. Please contact them right away.

● ____ neglected to send the ____'s. Could you get it done since ____'s locked in a meeting?

● The ____ in the computer malfunctioned. See what you can do, please. This is urgent.

Quick tip

Regardless of whether you're in a crisis, you're solving problems, or you're under a deadline, be precise. Let the recipients know exactly what happened, what they need to do, and when they need to do it. By the way—try not to give too much lead time. This can work against you, since people will forget. If you do, be sure to follow up as the time draws near.

Don't

● As soon as possible (when is that?)

● At your earliest convenience (it's never convenient)

● Whenever you can (that's just about never)

Do

● Immediately

● Within the hour

● By 5:00 today

Tight Deadline Because a Competitor Threatens to Launch a Product—or Open a New Business—Before You Do

Actually, this is the easiest deadline message to convey. It gives you an external force that pushes employees to action. It sets up a healthy, competitive racelike feeling, full of energy and charge. And it lets you know when you've won the race or didn't. Here are the phrases that push you out the starting gate.

When You Just Heard the News

Generally, you should follow this structure:

What you heard . . . What you must do to compete

- We just heard that _____. Let's see if we can get _____ going next week.
- _____ is going to introduce its new _____ early this summer. Let's get cranking and introduce ours on ____.
- _____ is planning to move into the _____. We better increase our presence there immediately. Let's get on the phone with PR.
- Just learned that _____ is about to _____. Let's contact advertising. We need a more aggressive campaign.

Here are some specific examples of how it might look:

- Just heard that Marshall's is going to open a new store in Boston this summer. We better hustle to finalize our agreement with the real estate developers so we can have our doors open in spring.
- RDIR is going to launch its new program in two weeks. Tell PR to get some press releases out so we can make a big splash right away.
- Just heard on the wire that EveryTech plans to put out a new version of its software. Are we ready to launch? See if R&D can speed up the pace.

When Your Team Is Moving Too Slowly

You can use the "If we don't, then . . ." strategy:

If we don't . . . then . . .

● If we don't finish ____ by May, then ___ will be on the market first.

● If we don't find an office soon, then ____ will tap into our market.

● If we don't finish developing the product, then we may be too late getting it on the shelves.

● If we don't get aggressive with our campaign, then we'll be buried by their advertising.

Or you can use an advantage-first approach, saying, "So we can . . ., we must . . ."

So we can . . ., we must . . .

● So we can get media attention, we must announce the product first.

● So we can get people to sign up, we must launch a door-to-door campaign next month.

● So we can get people to sign up with us, we must canvass the shopping malls before the holiday season.

Let the content determine which works to your advantage the most.

You Derail a Project and Must Explain to the Customer

Talk about grace under fire. You derailed the project, and the one who's most affected is your client. So you must show concern but not panic. Be apologetic but not humiliated. Act quickly without breaking into chaos. Phew. Now what? Follow up, to make sure your client forgives you and wants to move on.

Letting the Client Know

This requires strategy . . .

If . . . the problem is relatively easy to fix, say what you need to do, then why.

● We'll need to reinstall the ____ to get your ____ working again.

● We need to replace the ______, which should only take an hour, since the original burned out.

● We need to ____. This is simple to do, and your ____ should be up and running within an hour.

If . . . the problem will take time to fix, say what happened and how you can fix it:

- The ______ was not secure, so it slipped out of place. As a result, we will need to _____.
- Because the ad copy had several misspellings, we will need to redesign and print it again. This will take two additional weeks.
- We found that the _____ was the wrong size. We will need to construct and implement a new one.

When possible, show the advantage of your taking great care in repeating the steps. If possible, highlight the advantages:

- This will ensure that ______.
- As a result, the _____ will be even better than before we began.
- In the process, we will look for any _____.
- We will try to identify any _____ also, which will help you _____ in the future.
- As we go, we will note any _____ and get you that information. It will help you . . .

Avoid overly negative language. The situation is bleak; no need to make it bleaker.

Don't

- Unfortunately, you will not be able to_____ until we make these repairs.
- We were unable to ______.
- We cannot use the one we have now.
- You cannot begin until ______.

Do

- You will be able to_____ once we make these repairs.
- We still need to ______.
- We need to give you new ones.
- You can begin on ______.

When Offering Something Extra as Compensation

You should do this first when you contact them and later when you follow up.

Generally, you will use phrases like these:

- To make up for the delay, we will . . .
- Of course, we will not bill you for . . .
- We will add an extra ____ to your contract.
- In addition to the ____, we will send you a ____ as an apology.
- The ____ and the ____ normally cost $____. But we will only charge you ____ to cover the manufacturer's expense.

When Following Up on a Project You Derailed

No need to remind them of the problem—or apologize yet again. Instead, let them know what they're getting and that you promised it:

- As promised on ____, I am sending __________.
- Please note that we did not charge you for ___ or ___.
- In April, we said we would add another month to your contract without a fee. So we will continue your service without charge.
- You'll notice on line 5 of the invoice that we deducted _____ percent from your bill.

Because of New Requirements (Legal or Otherwise), You Must Redirect Your Employees, Your Paperwork, and Your Processes

Rules and regulations are hard enough for employees to abide by. Deviate, and a lawsuit may be pending. So you need to implement some quick project management strategies when new rules, regulations, and policy spring up. Why is this so hard? For one thing, people follow rules by habit. They do what they've always done. Now, suddenly, they have to change, which requires extra thought and energy and a certain amount of back stepping. So you need to make them snap to attention. Then, depending on the changes, you have morale to think about. Employees who are overworked have little patience for changes and may get discouraged.

Think of these perfect phrases as pick-me-ups that get them to pay attention and keep their spirits high as they do.

When Introducing New Rules and Regulations

Let them know who originated the changes—especially when your company has no involvement in them:

● The Department of ______ established these new regulations this fall.

● Because of changes to the _____, we must change our policies about _____.

● The ___ issued new guidelines for us to follow. I'm passing out copies for you to read.

● The requirements for all ___ have changed as of the 1st according to the ______. From now on, you must do the following: __________.

When Addressing Concerns

Show how you'll support them—be specific, even if you don't have precise times:

● We'll be holding seminars to teach you how to manage the new requirements. I don't know the dates yet, but will get back to you soon.

● The company has produced a manual that addresses your questions.

● You can take an online training session any time—even from your house.

Reassure people by letting them know help is available. Be specific, giving contact names, e-mail addresses, phone numbers, and, when necessary, the time they'll be available:

● You can contact ___ in the HR Department with questions any time from 8:00 to 5:00 at ext. ___.

● The Help Desk is fully prepared to answer your questions. You can call or e-mail the people there any time during the workweek.

● E-mail me if you are confused about what to do—or stop by my desk. As long as the door is open, come on in.

When Addressing Anger or Other Forms of Push-Back

● I know this seems difficult, but you'll get used to it soon.

● This will become habit in no time.

● Just relax—when we introduced the old procedures, everyone thought they were complex, and now they seem easy. The same will happen for you.

Questions You Should Ask Others if Uncertain About New Rules and Regulations

- What should I do if _____ occurs?
- How does this affect situations like ____ and _____?
- What was the reason why they changed the existing procedures?
- Whom should I talk to if I'm uncertain about legal ramifications?
- What kind of training will the company offer?
- Does everyone in the company have to follow these policies or just our department?
- How do we know if we're doing them wrong?

Make sure that you know how to address your customers' concerns by asking these questions:

- Do our clients know about the changes?
- What should we tell them if they ask why the procedures are different?
- Whom should we send the customers to if they have questions about these changes?
- What if our customers insist that we follow the previous steps?
- Do you have any information printed out that we can give them?

第七章

遭遇财务困境

处理财务问题时，一定要意识到：对人们（尤其是经商者）而言，财务不仅仅是数字，它关系到成就、名望、前途以及以往投资收益。更别提它还关系到自我、竞争、生活方式以及是否事业有成。财务混乱意味着生活一团糟。

所以如果发现自己被财务问题所困，一定要意识到情况万分危急。既要解决争议，又不能损害关系。要相信前途是光明的，只有拥有这种信念才能走出困境。

讨论财务问题，请记住以下原则。

- **保持客观，依据无争议的数字。**以书面协议、合同和文件为据。当然，前提是所有交易有具体法律文书，此方面请参考其他书目。
- **不要带感情色彩。**把情绪暂时放下，无论你是感到气愤、被伤害、被侮辱、沮丧还是恶心，只讨论是否公平。关注行动，你同意支付一定金额，对方许诺交换具体东西；你答应提供某种服务，对方同意在某天支付服务费用。
- **采取“向前看”方法。**记住，你是想找到一种解决方案，而不是赢得一场战斗。所以沟通的目的是要侧重于得到想要的结果，而不是赢得比赛或者证明自己的观点。

要是对方的确想敲诈（有时难免会发生），你最好在发第二条消息之前，拿起电话寻求法律援助。

你的团队预算花光了，必须对此给予解释

这真是个麻烦。你同意完成一定量的工作。你是专业人士，精确判断出工作所需的时间和耗材，甚至你还许诺会精打细算。然而……结果如何？情况有变，事与愿违。那么，最好运用以下完美措辞。

情况失控，造成麻烦

具体指出影响预算的因素。实际措辞视情况而定，但是可参考以下说法。

- 我方首次预算后，部分零件成本上涨 20%，因此需要更多的费用。
- 由于……需要额外支出，我方需要的法律诉讼费用大大超出预算。
- 由于……低迷，我方首轮投资亏损了。
- 我方从银行方面得到的资金数额减少了 15%，由此影响了最初的资金预算。

团队出错导致困境

承认错误。要清清楚楚，客观无误。请使用以下开头语。

- 我们低估了……的成本。
- 我们今年的预算是按照去年的成本做的。
- 我们低估了承包商完成该项目的工作时间。
- 我们高估了他们，以为能用有限资源完成那段项目工作。

对方有能力承担费用

- 你有多种方式可以承担此费用。我可以为你指出来。
- 我们会有不同的发展方向，要看你想要的结果以及你的时间安排。
- 我们不想敷衍了事，不过可以在成本控制上找到策略。
- 我知道你可以用一些方法削减额外开支，同时也能得到你预期的结果。

关键在于不要让他们缩减开支

你可以认同他们的观点，然后提醒他们不能减少投资的原因。

- 我理解你不愿再投资于此项目，但后果可能是……
- 我相信……这些钱看上去很多，但是如果你现在不投资的话，最终会花费更多。
- 正如我们所讨论的那样，此次预算意义重大。出于我们所议的原因，你必须追加投资，否则……会亏本。

或者直接切入正题。

- 要想这个项目最终盈利，你必须再投资________美元。
- 应该再增加投资，比你期望的多 25%。坦白说，我不想冒险。
- 完工的唯一方式是你再投入 2.5 万美元预算。

需要应急专款

在很多情况下都需要申请应急专款，主要是因为要办理大大小小的业务。你的措辞取决于资金来源和申请理由。当然，如果是申请商业贷款的话，最关键的还是你的资产。不管怎样，都可使用以下完美措辞。

你时间紧急，急需融资

- 为了……我们需要在本月 1 日前筹集________美元。
- 我们还差________美元，要在本月 15 日前……
- 我们本季度还差________（百分比），必须补齐差额。否则，我们收支会不相抵。
- 解决困难的唯一方式是迅速融资________美元。
- 如果我们在 5 月 1 日前能弄到________美元，就能结账。

当你发现难得的机遇，需要资金来抓住它

- 这个业务扩展时机非常难得，但是抓住它的条件是必须在下两周投

资________美元。

● 我们只有一丝机会确保交易成功，那就是投资________美元。最后日期是________

● 这个机会千载难逢，可以确保获益，但是需要筹集________美元。

● 要是下个月能筹集到________美元，我们能参加这项工程，收益将会很可观。

其他公司提出业务挑战

● 我们需要立即筹集________美元，弥补我公司可能遭到的损失。________发动了新的广告宣传活动，对我方不利。

● 我们需要向……再投资________美元，由于________威胁要研发一项专利。

● 我们需要至少________美元，用于加强员工基础，以便更好与________竞争那项价值百万元的项目。

市场变化需要你方投资新工序或新材料

提出你需要的具体金额，指明原因。

● 我们需要更新……以适应技术变化。这需要大概________美元融资。

● 目前市场要求……这需要大约________美元来推进下一步研发。

● 有________美元的投入，我们就能开发出一项……从而更大程度地满足市场需要。

发生灾难性事件，你被迫寻求资助

● 最近的飓风毁掉了我们的实验室，需要________美元用于灾后重建，购买新设备。

● 由于去年的火灾，我们被迫关闭工厂。为了重新开厂并雇佣现有的200名员工，我们需要________美元。

● 由于经济衰退，消费者在……方面的消费减少，这种情况出乎我们的意料。因此我们需要额外资金开发新业务。

你得知有员工窃取公司财物

无论你的态度如何，这种情况都令人厌恶。你必须阻止这种行为，完全是因为这么做是不对的，但是不要牵连到自己，甚至不要与此事有任何关联，也不要让你因此受到犯罪分子的报复。除此之外，你确定窃贼的身份吗？或许有多名员工参与其中。别着急！这些完美措辞有助于你弘扬正义，为公司节约资金，并取得你应得的胜利。

你不确定窃贼身份

你关注此事，想知道犯罪分子的真面目，但是更重要的是你想阻止盗窃行为。以下完美措辞能助你一臂之力。

在会议上

● 我发现公司的________已经丢失几个月了，可能时间更长。我无意指责他人，但很明显有人行窃。

● 每周会议结束后，我们都会缺失……我想大家都清楚注册登记资金开支情况。这一定是有人在其中做手脚。

● 我们必须讨论一件麻烦的重要事情：有人正在窃取公司财物。我知道……

在邮件中

● 请注意公司的________不翼而飞了。近几个月来，这种事情不断发生，我们只能推断是有人行窃。

● 我们发现有人拿走了________。必须立刻住手！你迟早会被抓住，到时候事情就麻烦了。

● 如果有人知道________的下落，请告知我或者保安。我们会对你的举报保密。

小提示

有时，诚实的人也会借工作之便中饱私囊。他们会以种种理由来为自己的行为辩护，比如公司供应充足，或者自己工资太低，既然如此，为何不顺手牵羊来弥补差距？想要让他们打消这种念头（尤其是你并不能确定对方身份时），方法很简单，你只需要把这种犯罪行为公布于众。那样的话他自然就会感到一丝羞愧，道德感便会油然而生。

知道窃贼身份，直接找对方对质

这种情况一定要谨慎。如果你弄错了，不但会造成严重伤害局面，而且双方关系将会产生无法估量的损害。即使你是对的，你也会遇到大麻烦。你必须弄清楚自己想要的结果，是想让对方老实承认？不大可能；对方百般抵赖？这倒是很有可能。但是至少让对方明白：自己已经暴露了。因此除非你人赃并获，否则最好的方式还是旁敲侧击。

- 我发现钱从……不翼而飞了，你知道可能会到哪儿去了吗？
- 昨天，我看见你把________放进包里。如果我弄错了，向你道歉。但是我想指出来那是偷窃行为。
- 我无意中听说你告诉________，你拿走了……你一定清楚这是偷窃行为。这件事，________也应该受到指责，他应该举报你。

你确定窃贼身份，应该报告上司

你应该表明自己不愿意告发他人。你与该员工本无瓜葛，但是正义感促使你阻止这种行窃行为。

- 我不愿提起这件事，但是……
- 您知道，我与________关系十分融洽。但我想说的内容与私交无关。
- ________在很多方面都特别优秀，但是最近我亲眼所见……
- 我很犹豫是否应该把这件事告诉您，但是我认为应该这样做。
- 我想向您报告一件重要的事情，但是很难开口……

小提示

先直接说出事实真相，没有时间猜测，尽量准确无误。请牢记：如果你认为自己看到了发生的事情，但是不能确定，一定要等待。即使只是怀疑某人做坏事，这也会毁掉对方的名誉。

不要猜测

- 我觉得我看到他……
- 我认为他很可能……
- 我看到他经过现金出纳机时，四处张望。
- 我觉得他会那样做。
- 我听说他以前出过此类问题。

一定要确定

- 我看见他拿了现金，放进自己的口袋。
- 储存柜里的东西变少了，只有他一个人有此柜的钥匙。
- 他向我承认他拿走了相关物资，并将其倒卖掉了。

员工在你面前讨论所盗物件

- 我认为这太糟糕了。这种行为毫无道德可言，是完全非法的。你必须立即住手。
- 有人可能觉得无所谓，但是我可不这么认为。我认为你至少应该停止干那种事了，而最好能在业务上有所作为以弥补损失。
- 我知道你会认为顺手牵羊在这种情况下是可以接受的，但是偷窃就是偷窃，这种行为是完全不对的。

员工或承包商吹嘘索要高价获利

- 你应该按照合同的规定索要价格。
- 许多承包商要价过高。这是不对的，你不能这么干。
- 要么你正常要价，否则的话，我会采取行动的。
- 你的行为不仅错误，而且非法。那些获悉此事却保持沉默的人也应受到谴责。

心仪的客户拖欠款项，你无法与对方交易

该客户一直表现良好，他是长期顾客，既讨人喜欢，付款也及时。但是对方目前陷入困境，拖欠的服务款项日积月累，实在令人沮丧。你不愿意这么做，但是你不得不中止与他的业务关系。不过，情况复杂，你的客户也许会时来运转，所以你不想永远失去对方。除此之外，你不想使该客户在行业内的名声受损。你与对方刚刚建立信任，不想放弃。应该如何应对这种情况？相信以下完美措辞能帮你渡过难关。

让你的客户知道你必须中止其业务

有可能的话，向其解释中止业务关系是一项公司决议，而非个人成见。

● 您知道您是我最喜爱的客户之一，但是公司政策规定不得向拖欠款项的客户提供服务。

● 我真希望能继续成为贵方的……但是很抱歉，您必须付清所欠款项。

● 多年来您一直是我方最稳定的客户，深得全公司的喜爱和敬重。如果我负责此事，我会继续为您提供服务，但是我方财务部门禁止我违规操作。

如果你已经尽力而为，并且破例行事，请务必让你的客户对此领情。这样做有利于维系关系，一旦该客户时来运转，就会有再次合作的可能。

● 按规定如果客户有两次付款未到位，我们必须中止合作关系。如您所知，我们已经对贵方网开一面了。

● 如有顾客欠款超过 1 个月，公司就会要求我们联系法律事务部，但对于您的情况，我方愿意再宽限一段时间。

努力达成协议

● 如果愿意，贵方可以选择分期付款。

● 我愿意减免 15% 的账单金额，用以帮助贵方结清账目。

如可能，让对方承担责任，做出可行的合理安排。

- 您想如何安排支付日程?
- 您认为贵方何时可以付款?
- 您想制定付款计划吗?

与内部人员谈论该客户

你不能再提供服务了，同事对此事一清二楚，但是你不想让客户留下恶名，因此你必须诚实而又谨慎。当同事询问该项目是否继续开展，或者停工的原因时，请使用以下完美措辞。

- 目前，他们无法继续开工。
- 他们因……需要休息。准备再开工时会通知我们。
- 他们因……受到严重影响，必须撤掉目前接受的服务。
- 他们转型有段时间了，正关注其他活动。

同你方账务部门提及此事

- 我们需要调整账务周期。
- 在账务方面，我们或许可以与他们算账。
- 你能同他们讨论账目问题吗?我们可能需要算出金额，以便他们能付款。
- 你认为我们能否制定出付款方案，以便减少他们所欠我方债务?

现金流转出现问题，你被迫推迟支付员工和承包商的工资

在此类沟通中，你需要处理各种问题。显然，最佳方式是尽量争取不发生此类事件。但是常言道，是福不是祸，是祸躲不过。所以你必须向所有员工保证：你不会赖账，一定会付清欠款。你需要逐步完善付款方案，并按时发放工资，才能维持住大家的信心。最后一点，你务必要传递出这种信息：你力量强大，局面尽在掌控之中。这样所有员工才会对你的公司、

你的奋斗目标和愿景充满信心。

通知员工工资要拖欠

可以对拖欠工资表达个人歉意。你对此感到难过，希望员工们理解。首先通知坏消息。

- 不幸的是，大家这周的工资不能全额发放。
- 由于现金流问题，我只能发放部分工资。我想支付全额，但是目前无能为力。
- 很抱歉我只能支付你们正常工资的一半。

然后，告知对方你的弥补措施。

- 本周我会支付你们……下次发薪日将全额发放。
- 我会把差额工资分三期付款补齐，日期分别是______、______和______。
- 我没有预计会出现问题，但我会于______付清全额工资。
- 我制定了这个付款方案，你们可以弄清楚事情的进展。

解释困境产生的原因

如果责任不在他们，那么具体解释内容的细节视实际情况而定。可以参考以下措辞。

- 近来我们失去了最大的客户，因此，现在现金流发生短缺。
- 由于我们的开支急剧上升，因此在维护日常职责方面出现了问题。
- 由于市场转移，我们的客户比以前减少了。
- 很多客户拖欠我们的款项，因此……

员工造成了目前的困境。

- 由于你们两个月没有给我开账单了，尽管我一直跟进，但现在我无法付清你们全部的报酬。
- 由于修改你给客户的报告以及其他几个错误，造成目前我们无法按时发薪。
- 由于……发生故障后，客户找到了新卖方。现在现金流出现了中断。

树立乐观意识

你不做任何许诺，也不能兑现什么，你无法确切预料事态的发展，不过尽量保持乐观的心态，积极向上。

错误说法：

- 我们本周末资金会到位。
- 我们本月一定能赢得几个很好的合同。
- 我们正期待……的巨大胜利。
- 我刚获悉，________ 告知我们，那个账户现在可以使用了。

正确说法：

- 我相信本月我们会赢得几笔大的合同。
- 我们很可能本月底会收到几笔支票款项。
- 我们正在努力奋斗赢取________和________两笔账目，真不知道哪笔入账更好。
- 目前我们制定出一些可靠的方案。
- 只要大家努力奋斗，斗志高昂，很快就会财源滚滚来。

由于现金流转问题，你必须让客户提前付款

这种困境不只是发展不力。你要请同行私下帮忙，甚至更糟糕的是，可能会请客户帮忙。同时，你不想让客户轻视你，认为你处于弱势。但是你的确需要资金，想让对方知道你对他们的努力感激不尽。以下完美措辞和注意事项一定能帮上忙。

要求预付部分或全额款项

若你有很好的业绩记录。

- 能否请您预先支付估算金额的 25%？这样能帮助我们解决一些现

金流问题。如您所知，在双方业务往来的十年中，我方一直为您提供优质服务。

- 我们会 22 一如既往地提供……只是这次希望贵方能预付部分或全部费用。

注意：你不必告诉客户你现金流转出了问题，即使对方很可能会表示理解。提醒客户签订协议，有助于确保你方提供相关商品或服务。

- 按照惯例，我们会遵守合同的相关规定。
- 我们会按照项目计划的时间规定，为贵方提供切实的服务。
- 如协议规定，你方会于________收到……

不要由于要求客户预付款项而向其许诺额外服务或更好的时间，这样更像是贿赂。另外，为什么就不能让客户每次都如此呢?

如果你有先期投入。

- 希望贵方能先付全额的 25%，支付……费用。我们一般不这么要求客户，但是这次，我们将对此感激不尽。
- 能否先付________美元购买……这样就能给我们很大的帮助。
- 由于你的方案需要一大笔预付费用，我们希望你方立刻支付________美元。

在付账期限内要求预付费用

- 我方要求贵方支付我方于……提供的……费用。能否早点付账?
- 我知道贵方支票周转期是 60 天。这次可否采用……支付方式？其周转期只有 30 天。
- 这次可否早点支付最新账单？账单编号是________，日期是________。
- 如可能，请尽快支付________号账单。本人将感激不尽。

小提示

如果你与客户关系很熟，有私交，你可以说“希望您帮忙……”，或者让客户了解本月你手头有点紧。另外，如果情况岌岌可危，不要告诉对方，避免使用“情况糟糕”和“问题严重”这类言语。

要求支付到期账单

具体指出涉及细节，让客户明确你希望他支付的账单是哪一张。

- 请发给我们支票支付_______号账单。这是一笔有关我方于_______提供_______服务的费用，该账单于_______日到期。
- 请告知我方收到支票的时间，该支票用于支付我方于_______提供的_______服务。我们希望于_______收到这笔款项，但是一直没收到。
- 我们开了账单，贵方须支付于……收到的_______号账单。贵方当时同意于_______付款，但是我方至今未收到。请问何时到账？

小提示

顺便提一下，即使你对拖欠支票很生气，也要注意说话语气。拖欠款项一两周可能是疏忽，也可能是现金流转或预算出现问题。你当然不想疏远宝贵的客户，丢掉眼前的一大笔生意。

你目前工资收支不相抵，需要争取加薪

你的上司不是你的朋友，对方没有义务帮你摆脱困境，因此你必须采取完全专业和正规的方法获得加薪。首先要弄清以下问题。

- 我是否应得到加薪？
- 和我职位相同的人工资是否比我多？
- 公司政策在年限上是否支持我加薪？（如果你在公司供职时间过短，加薪要求是不予考虑的。）

如果对于以上三个问题，你的答案都是肯定的，接着再问自己下列问题。当你要求上涨工资时，下面这些问题的答案会决定你所采用的完美措辞。

- 我加薪最重要的三个原因是什么？
- 和我同级的员工都挣多少？
- 如果我现在的表现已经很出色了，那么我的工作在哪些方面为公司赢利做出了贡献？这正是我加薪的理由。

然后面见上司。视情况而定，你可以发邮件给对方。不过最好坐下来面议此事。但是，不要贸然去见上司。与对方约定时间，让他能真正聆听你的意见，并给予答复。

发邮件提出当面交谈

让老板明白交谈时间很短，内容积极。

- 我们能谈一会儿吗？最多 15 到 20 分钟，谈谈我对公司的贡献。
- 我想下周同您面谈。周一早晨方便拜访吗？
- 我想同您谈谈我在公司的作用。我会同________联系，确定过几天能否安排一次简短的面谈。

要求加薪

不要咄咄逼人，让上司明白你很看重对方的决策。

错误说法：

- 我认为我应该得到加薪。
- 我相信我努力工作，该得到加薪了。
- 我想在公司多挣点钱。
- 我是一名优秀员工，一直得到大家好评，理应得到加薪。

正确说法：

- 我想您是否能考虑给我加薪？

- 我想讨论一下我的贡献，希望您会考虑给我加薪。
- 我希望公司给我加薪。过去 6 个月里，我的业绩非常突出。

提供依据

你必须具体说明。如果你认为自己工作努力，为什么你的上司或经理应该重视你？顾客是否也认可你？你的兢兢业业取得了业绩吗？或者你只是忙于无用的活动？不要指望你老板会知道这些细节，你必须提醒对方。

错误说法：

- 我工作十分努力。
- 客户喜欢我。
- 我工作一直很认真，我总是尽善尽美。
- 我工作尽忠职守。

正确说法：

- 我一直早上 8 点钟上班，下午 5 点钟下班。
- 在客户满意度调查中，我名列前茅。事实上，95% 的客户给我的评分为“优秀”。
- 我找出了账单存在的问题，这每年为公司挽回了________美元的损失。
- 通过网上业务，我招募的求职者数量比前任大幅增长。

确保展示你的业绩

- 结果，我们________没有一人迟到。
- 我开始监管提案后，我们的业务量比去年增加了 20%。
- 这让我能……这也是我能够……的原因。
- 我们的人员招聘率和保留率比以往增加了 25%。

加薪要求遭到拒绝

找出原因，明白你应该改进的地方，再继续努力。

- 想要加薪，我该如何努力?
- 我是否应该注重某方面的工作业绩，以增加我给公司创造的价值?
- 我如何能提高业绩?
- 您会依据什么因素来决定是否给员工加薪?

Part Seven

Difficult Financial Situations

When addressing financial matters, be aware that for everyone—but especially those in business—finance is about more than numbers. It's about success, reputation, the future, and the payback of the past. Not to mention, ego, competitiveness, lifestyle, and a general sense of doing well—or not—in the world. Mess with people's finances and you've messed with a lot!

So if you find yourself engaged in a financial entanglement, remember that beneath your feet lie beds of hot, white coals. You need to settle your dispute without jeopardizing your relationship, and leave that difficult situation with a sense that the one ahead will be brighter and clear.

So when discussing financial matters, remember these perfect pointers:

● Be objective. Rely on unambiguous numbers backed up in paper by an agreement, a contract, or a written document. Of course, that assumes all your interactions are based on concrete and legal written documents, but that's for another book.

● Discard emotion. Put aside any emotions—whether you're angry, hurt, insulted, frustrated, or disgusted. And limit your discussion of what is or isn't fair. Instead, focus on actions: You agreed to pay a certain amount. They promised to give something concrete back in return. You promised and provided a service. They agreed to pay for it by a specific date.

● Keep a forward-looking approach. Remember, you want to figure out a solution, not win a battle. So your communications must be focused on getting a result, not winning a competition or making a point.

Should they really want to rip you off (well, it does happen), then better pick up the phone and get some legal backing before you send another message.

Your Team Went Over Budget, and You Must Explain Why

This really is a problem. You agreed to do a certain amount of work and, experts that you are, gauged exactly how much it would cost for time and materials. Even better, you promised to squeeze out the value of every dollar. Then . . . guess what? Something happened; things changed. Better pull out these perfect phrases.

When Circumstances Beyond Your Control Caused the Problem

Be specific about the factors that affected your budget. The actual word use, of course, depends on your situation, but would look something like this:

- Because the cost of parts went up by 20 percent from the time we first drafted the budget, we need more money.
- We had to pay higher legal expenses than we anticipated because the ____ required additional costs.
- Because of the ______slump, we lost money in our initial round of investments.
- The figures that we received from the bank were off by 15 percent. This affected the budget we originally drafted.

When a Mistake on Your Team's Part Caused the Problem

Confess—clearly and in the most objective terms. Here are some opening phrases:

- We underestimated the costs of . . .
- We used last year's costs to determine this year's budget.
- We underestimated the amount of time it would take the contractors to complete that phase of the project.
- We overestimated their ability to complete that phase of the project with limited resources.

When the Other Party Has Options to Contain the Costs

- You have numerous options that can help contain the costs. Let me outline them for you.
- We can take different directions depending on the outcome and the timing you have in mind.
- We don't want to cut corners, but we can strategize ways of limiting the costs.
- I know a few ways you can cut additional costs and still have the outcomes you intended.

When It's Critical That They Don't Scrimp on Spending

You can acknowledge their perspective and then say why they shouldn't take financial shortcuts:

- I understand that you'd rather not invest more on this project, but the result could be that . . .
- I'm sure that ___ more money seems like a lot, but ultimately you'll spend much more money if you don't make the investment now.
- The budget made a lot of sense when we first discussed it. But for the reasons we discussed, you must add to it, or the _____ could be a loss.

Or get directly to the point:

- You need to invest ___ more dollars if you want the project to ultimately bring in a profit.
- The right parts cost 25 percent more than what you want to spend, but frankly, I wouldn't take the gamble.
- The only way we can complete the project is if you add $25,000 to your budget.

You Need Unexpected Funding

There are lots of possibilities for getting emergency funding, mainly because businesses large and small are so frequently in need. Whom you get your money from and why will dictate the content of your message. Of course, if you're getting

a business loan, what matters most is your assets. But one way or another, you'll probably need these perfect phrases.

When You're under a Time Crunch and Need a Quick Financial Infusion

● In order to ______, we need $ _____ by the first of the month.

● We are short $____ and need to ______ by the 15th of the month.

● We were under by ___percent this quarter and need to make up the difference, or we won't be able to keep up with expenses.

● The only way we can overcome this setback is to get a quick infusion of $_____.

● If we get $____ by May 1, we will be able to make our payments.

When You Discover an Opportunity You Must Seize and Need the Capital to Do So

● The opportunity for growth is amazing, but only if we get $____ within the next two weeks.

● We have a really narrow window to cinch the deal and need $____ to do it. Our drop-dead deadline is ______.

● This is a remarkable opportunity, and the gains are undeniable. But we need to raise $____ to achieve it.

● If we can raise $____ within the next month, we can participate in this project. The returns potential is highly positive.

When Another Company or Business Is Challenging Your Business

● We need to raise $____ immediately to offset the potential damage ____ can cause to our company through their new negative advertising campaign.

● We need to invest $ _____ into our ____, as ____ threatens to develop an exclusive patent.

● We need at least $_____ to ramp up our employee base and effectively compete with ____ for the multimillion-dollar project.

When Changes in the Market Require That You Invest in New Processes or Materials

State how much you need and the forces that require you get it:

- We need to update our ___ to keep up with technology changes in the ____. This will require an infusion of funding of approximately $____.
- The market is now demanding ____. This will cost us approximately $___ to get our R&D efforts to the next step.
- With $____ of seed money, we will be able to develop a ___ that more than meets market need.

When a Devastating Event Forces You to Seek Financial Backing

- We lost our labs in the recent hurricane. We will need $____ to repair the damages and buy new equipment.
- Owing to the fire last year, we needed to close our factories. To reopen them, and employ as many of our 200 employees who are still available, we will need $______.
- Because of the recession, consumer spending on ____ like ours has sunk beyond anyone's expectations. We need additional funding to develop the ___ component of our business.

You Learn Some of the Employees Are Stealing from the Company

This situation stinks no matter how you look at it. You need to stop the action simply because it's wrong. Yet you cannot incriminate yourself—even by association. Nor should you leave yourself vulnerable to attack should the culprit want revenge. Besides, do you really know who the thief is? Perhaps more than one employee is in on it. But don't worry. These perfect phrases will help you play the good guy, save your company money, and come up on top—where you belong.

When You're Unsure Who Is Stealing

You're concerned. Sure, you want to know who the culprit is. But more, you want the stealing to end. These phrases should help that happen.

In a Meeting

● I have come to realize that ____ has been missing from the company for several months, maybe longer. I don't want to blame any one person, but clearly someone here has been stealing.

● We have been short at least ____ every week after closing. I want all of you to be aware of how much money comes and goes from the register, as someone is quite clearly stealing.

● We need to discuss an important but difficult matter: someone is stealing from the company. Here's how I know . . .

In an E-Mail

● Please be aware that _____ has been missing from the company. Since this problem has been reoccurring for months now, we can only assume that someone is stealing.

● We are aware that someone has been taking the ____.

You need to stop this behavior at once. Eventually you will get caught, and the situation will be difficult for all of us.

● If any of you knows how our _____ has vanished, please let me, or someone in security, know. Whatever you say will be kept confidential.

Quick tip

Sometimes otherwise honest people find themselves stealing at work. They justify the action, telling themselves the company has more than enough supplies, or they're underpaid so why not steal a little something to make up the difference. Getting them to stop—especially when you don't know exactly who they are—can be as simple as bringing the crime to everyone's attention. Then an element of shame, and decency, will creep in.

When You Know Who Is Stealing and Confront Him or Her Directly

Be careful here. If you're wrong, you will create a seriously injurious situation and ruin a relationship beyond measure.

If you're right, and you need to be dead certain, then you should be clear about the outcome you expect. A confession? Unlikely. A denial? Probably. But at least the person will know he or she is being watched. So unless you've caught the person red-handed, an indirect approach may be the best one possible:

- I've noticed that money has been missing from the _____. Would you know where it went?
- Yesterday, I saw you put ____ in your bag. If I am mistaken, I apologize, but I did want to point out that is stealing.
- I overheard you tell _____ that you took _____. This is stealing, as I'm sure you know. And at this point, ____ is equally to blame for not turning you in.

When You Know Who Is Stealing and Need to Tell Your Boss

Be clear that you are not comfortable being a snitch and have nothing against the employee personally. But you couldn't let the thefts continue with a clear conscience.

- I feel uncomfortable bringing this up, but ...
- As you know, _____ and I have gotten along quite well, so what I'm about to say is not personal.
- _____ is a really good employee in many ways. But I recently witnessed him ...
- I really debated whether or not I should tell you this, but I know it's the right thing to do.
- I need to tell you something that is important but difficult to discuss ...

Quick tip

Get your facts straight—this is no time for speculation. Then be as clear and accurate as possible. Remember: If you think you saw something but aren't sure—wait. Even a suggestion of wrongdoing could hurt that person's reputation.

Do Not Speculate

- I believe I saw her ...

- It looked to me as though he . . .
- I noticed that she was glancing around after passing the cash register.
- It strikes me that he is the type to do that.
- I heard she has been in trouble before.

Do Be Definitive

- I saw her take the cash and put it in her pocket.
- The supply cabinet has been low lately, and he is the only one with a key to it.
- She admitted to me that she takes the supplies and resells them.

When Employees Discuss the Items They Steal in Front of You

- I think that's a bad idea: it's immoral and illegal, and you should stop immediately.
- Some people may think that's okay, but I don't. I think you should stop at the least and reimburse the business at best.
- I know you don't think there's anything wrong with stealing in this situation—but stealing is stealing, and it's wrong.

When Employees or Contractors Brag About Overcharging

- You should only be charging the amount you agreed to in your contract.
- Lots of contractors overcharge, but it's still wrong, and you need to stop.
- Either you start billing correctly, or I'll do something about it.
- What you're doing is wrong and illegal. Those of you who know about it and don't say anything are equally to blame.

You Can't Sell to a Favored Client Because His Back Payments Are Long Overdue

Yes, at one time this client was great: regular, agreeable, and quick with the payments. But he or she has fallen into hard times, and the unpaid bill for your services has grown depressingly long. You hate to do it, but you need to cut the client off. But the situation is more complex. Your client's luck will probably shift, and you don't want to lose him or her for good. Besides, you don't want to hurt the client's reputation—even within your organization. You just have an allegiance, and you can't let go. So what do you do? Trust these perfect phrases to help.

When Letting Your Client Know You Must Cut Him or Her Off

Where possible, explain that cutting him or her off is a business decision—nothing personal:

● As you know, you're one of my favorite clients. But company policy states that we can't provide services to customers with outstanding bills.

● I wish I could continue to be your ____. But you need to pay off the amount you owe. I'm sorry.

● Over the years, you've been a steady and agreeable client. If it were up to me, I'd continue providing services. But our Financial Department won't let me make exceptions to our policy.

If you've gone out of your way and have, say, stretched the rules, make sure your client knows. This may help to secure a bond once the client's fortunes have changed.

● Normally, we need to cut clients off after they've missed two payments. In your case, as you know, we far exceeded that.

● The company requires us to contact our Legal Department should customers delay paying their bill for over a month. In your case, I'm willing to wait.

When Trying to Make a Deal

● If you like, you can pay small amounts over a few months until the whole bill is paid off.

● I'd be willing to deduct 15 percent from your bill if that will help you pay it off.

When possible, get them to take responsibility, and find a reasonable arrangement that will work for them:

● What kind of payment schedule would work for you?

● When do you think you'll be able to pay your bill?

● Would you like to suggest a payment plan?

When Speaking with Internal People About the Client

You can't continue providing services, and your coworkers should know this. But you don't want to brand the client forever. So you need to be honest but discreet. So when coworkers ask whether the project will continue or why it's stopped, use these perfect phrases:

- They're not in a position to continue right now.
- They need to take a break from the ____. They'll let us know when they're ready to start again.
- They got hit by the ______ pretty hard and need to pull back on the services they're receiving.
- They're changing course for a while and focusing on other efforts.

When Speaking with Your Billing Department

- We need to adjust their billing cycle.
- Perhaps we could work something out with them regarding bills.
- Could you speak to them about their bills? We may need to work something out so they can pay us.
- Do you think we could create a payment plan so they can eliminate their debt to us?

You Have to Delay Your Employees' and Contractors' Pay Because of Cash Flow Problems

You have numerous issues to address in this type of communication. Obviously, your best bet is to ensure you're not in this difficult position in the first place. But as the cliché goes, these things happen. So you need to assure the employees that you're not the bad guy and will, indeed, pay up. And you must sustain their confidence by working up a plan where you pay them the back amount and continue with your payments moving forward. Finally, you must project a message that you are strong and in control, so they have confidence in your company, your mission, and your vision.

Letting the Employees Know That Paychecks Will Be Delayed

It's okay to express personal regret about having to delay paychecks. You feel bad about this and want the employees to know it.

First let them know the bad news:

● Unfortunately, I won't be able to pay you the full amount this week.

● Because of cash flow problems, I have to limit your paychecks. I wish I could pay you the full amount, but right now I can't.

● I'm sorry to say that I can only pay you half of your normal check this cycle.

Then tell them what you will do for them:

● I will pay you ____ this week and the full amount the next pay cycle.

● I will make up the difference in three installments on ___, ___, and ____.

● I do not foresee any problems ahead and will have paid off the full amount on ___.

● I developed this payment plan so you know what to expect moving ahead.

Explaining Why the Situation Happened

When they're blameless, the specifics will depend on your situation, but should look like this:

● As you know, we lost our biggest client recently. So our cash flow is pretty low right now.

● Since our expenses have skyrocketed, we have had trouble keeping up with our usual responsibilities.

● Because of the market shift, we have fewer clients than before.

● Our clients are considerably overdue in their payments to us.

When something they did created the situation:

● Because you did not bill me for two months, although I kept following up, I cannot pay you the full amount right now.

● As a result of having to revise your report for the client—and several other glitches—we are not getting our own payments in on time.

● Because the client went with another vendor after the ____ malfunctioned, we don't have the cash flow, as before.

Project a Sense of Moving Forward

True, you shouldn't promise anything you can't deliver or commit to anything you can't predict for certain. But be as optimistic and forward-looking as possible.

Don't

- We're getting money in by the end of the week.
- We're definitely going to win some great contracts this month.
- I'm looking forward to some big wins on the ___ and ___.
- I just know ____ will tell us to get started on that account.

Do

- I'm hopeful that we'll win several big contracts this month.
- Most likely, we'll get several checks in by the end of the month.
- We're working hard to win the ___ and ___ accounts: I can't imagine who would be better.
- We have some solid proposals out there now.
- Everyone's working hard and has great spirits; the money should start flowing in!

You Need to Ask Clients to Send Their Payments Early Because of Cash Flow Issues

This situation can create less than perfect dynamics. You need to ask a business associate, even worse, a client, to do you a personal favor. At the same time, you don't want your client to see you as weak or vulnerable. Yet you really need the money and want the person to know how much you'll appreciate his or her efforts. These perfect phrases, and the dos and don'ts, should prove helpful.

When Asking for an Advance Partial or Full Payment

When you have a positive track record:

- Would you be able to pay 25 percent of the estimate up front? This would help us with some cash flow issues. As you know, we've always provided great service in the 10 years we've been doing business.
- As always, we'll provide the same ___ as we always have. Only, this time I was hoping you could pay some or all of the expense up front.

Note: You don't have to tell the client that you're having cash flow issues. Most likely, he or she will understand. When helpful, remind the client of an agreement

that will guarantee you'll provide the product or service:

- As always, we'll abide by the stipulations in our contract.
- We will provide you with the precise services within the time frame in our project plan.
- As our letter of agreement states, you will receive ____ on _____.

Do not promise the client an extra service or better timing for up-front payment. This will seem like bribery. Besides, why shouldn't the client get that special deal every time, regardless?

When you have up-front expenses:

- I was hoping you could pay 25 percent to cover the ____ expenses. We usually don't ask you, but this time, we would appreciate the effort.
- Could you send us $_____ to cover the ____ and _____? This will help us tremendously.
- Since your project requires a considerable amount of up-front costs, we were hoping you could send us $______ right away.

When Asking for a Payment within Days of Billing

- We just billed you for the ____ and _____ that we provided on _____. Could you possibly pay us early?
- I know that you usually have a 60-day turnaround for checks. But do you think you could pay us on _____, which is within 30 days, this time?
- Would you be able to pay the recent bill, number _____, dated _____, early this time?
- If possible, could you pay bill number _____ relatively soon? I'd be most appreciative.

Quick tip

If you have a strong, personal relationship with a client, it's okay to say things like "I was hoping you could do me a favor and . . ." Or let the client know that you're a bit squeezed this month. Still, if your situation feels dire, keep that to yourself and avoid terms like "terrible situation" or "dire problems."

When Asking for Payment of a Bill That's Overdue

Be specific so the client knows exactly which bill you mean and when you were expecting it to be paid:

● Could you please send us a check for bill number ____ regarding the ____ services we provided on ____. It was due on ____.

● Please let us know when we will receive a check for the ____ services that we provided on ____. We expected the payment on ____ but never received it.

● We sent a bill for the ____ that you received on ____. At that time, you agreed to pay us on ____, but we haven't received a check. When do you think you'll send it?

Quick tip

By the way, even if you're annoyed with a late check, watch your tone. A payment that's a week or two late could be an oversight or the result of cash flow or budget issues. Certainly, you don't want to alienate a perfectly good client and lose the good business that lies ahead.

You Can't Make Ends Meet on Your Current Salary and Need to Push Hard for a Raise

Your employer isn't your friend, nor is he or she in any way obliged to bail you out when times are tough. So you need to take a purely professional and businesslike approach when trying to get a raise. Your first step is to ask yourself these questions:

● Do I really deserve a raise?

● Are other people in my position getting more money than I am getting?

● Does company policy support the timeliness of my getting a raise? (For example, if you've only been working at the company for a short period, it won't even consider the request.)

If the answer to all three of these questions is yes, then ask yourself these follow-up questions. The answers will feed the perfect phrases you use when asking for that bump-up in your salary:

- What are the three most important reasons why I should get a raise?
- How much more are other people in my position getting?
- If I'm pretty much at the status quo, how do my activities benefit the company's bottom line—which will entitle me to an increase?

Then go ahead and confront your boss. Depending on your situation, you might want to e-mail him or her. But it's always best to sit down and discuss in a meeting. Don't just knock on the door and sit down in your boss' office, though. Set a time so he or she can really listen to your case and respond to it.

When E-Mailing for a One-on-One Meeting

Let your boss know the meeting will be short and positive:

- Could we have a short meeting, 15 or 20 minutes at most, where we could discuss my contributions to the company?
- I would like to meet with you next week. May I stop by on Monday morning?
- I'd like to talk with you about my role in the company. I'll contact _____ to see about scheduling a short meeting over the next few days.

When Asking for a Raise

Don't be pushy. Let your boss know that you value his or her role as a decision maker.

Don't

- I think I deserve a raise.
- I believe I am a hard worker and it's time for me to have a raise.
- I'd like to get more money for the work I'm doing here.
- I'm a good employee, and people compliment me all the time. So I think I am entitled to a raise.

Do

- I wonder if you would consider giving me a raise.
- I wanted to discuss my contributions with the hope that you'll consider giving me a raise.

- I was hoping the company would increase my pay because of the results I've been able to achieve over the last six months.

Provide Evidence

You must be specific. If you think you're a hard worker, why should your boss or manager care? Does the customer agree? Has your hard work brought results, or are you busily creating useless activity? Don't expect your boss to know any of this; you must remind him or her.

Don't

- I'm a really hard worker.
- The clients love me.
- I always try to do a good job; if anything, I'm a perfectionist.
- I am unusually qualified for the job.

Do

- I usually arrive at 8:00 and leave at 5:00.
- Client ratings about my service have been high: in fact, 95 percent gave me a score of "excellent."
- I have caught glitches in our billing, amounting to well over $_____ annually.
- Through my network, I have reached significantly more job seekers than my predecessors.

Be sure to show the results of your efforts:

- As a result, not one of our _____ has been late.
- After I started overseeing the proposals, we won 20 percent more work than this time last year.
- This allows me to _____, which is why I have been able to _____.
- We have a 25 percent higher recruitment and retention rate than before.

When You Get Turned Down for a Raise

Find out why. Learn what you can do. And come back again.

- What can I do to get a raise?

- Should I be focusing on any particular aspect of my performance to improve my value to the company?
- How can I become a better performer?
- What are the attributes you look for when determining whether to increase an employee's salary?

第八章

两性关系的沼泽

毫无疑问，不能在工作时间谈情说爱，也不能在工作时间上网看色情电影或者是给心上人发电子邮件。但是，我们都是正常人对吧？事实上，不对。工作期间我们必须把一部分人类的本性放在一边（至少是暂时放在一边），这样才能保证事业成功。事实上，职场上的罗曼蒂克就像是粘在脚上的橡皮糖，制约着我们前进，并且可能会带来巨大的麻烦。

但是，如果确实在职场上被爱神之箭射中了，该怎么办呢？对正在迷恋你的同事该说些什么呢？如何面对那些不期而至的献殷勤（某个站在复印机旁的家伙的挑逗或者老板送的鲜花和糖果）呢？对此视而不见显然是愚蠢的、不太可能的甚至是根本不可能的。以下是一些需要遵循的要点以及必备的完美措辞。

- **衡量干扰的程度。**各种职场罗曼蒂克的严重程度不同，要根据所涉及的不同情况进行应对。拒绝一次约会是一回事，如果对方继续纠缠那就严重了。如果此人尾随你回家、给你发邮件，或是在你经过时飞吻的话，那就是骚扰了。当然，那些在休息区大谈自己罗曼史的员工同样会造成不良影响。所以，要衡量干扰的程度，并且据此作出应对。

- **通过正确的渠道汇报。**有些情况下（也许是多数情况下），你需要向某一位权威人士反映此问题，但是要小心地选择向何人汇报。如果你是一位女员工，而你的老板是男性，当你向他投诉有男性员工骚扰你时，他可能会无动于衷。同样的，如果你向某位经理（无论是男是女）反映，对方很有可能不知道你该采取什么行动。在采取行动之前，你应该去咨询人事部门，甚至可以去咨询律师。

● **明确自己想要的结果。**你想得到什么样的结果呢？是要制止这一行为？把那个家伙调到另外的办公地点或是让他彻底消失？你是否真的认为该员工应受到更严厉的惩罚甚至被起诉？必须理清自己的思想和感情，以明确自己究竟想达到什么目的。所以，在与任何人沟通之前，要清楚地了解自己的想法。

两名员工之间关系暧昧

好吧，员工之间有了恋情，或者是有了奸情，谁知道呢？而且，坦白地说，这与你无关，也与他人无关，除非他们太张扬——比如眉来眼去、卿卿我我以及在停车场上的不雅举止。如果这些是发生在校园里，那没什么关系。但这里不是校园，并且他们的行为影响到了团队中的所有人。所以，他们最好低调一点。以下这些完美措辞一定会有所帮助。

与当事人之一谈话

● 如果你和________在工作之外彼此有好感的话，请做得更隐秘一点。

● 请你们工作结束之后再去说笑，在工作时间里这些吵闹会影响其他人。

● 在工作场合，你和________应该尽量把关系保持为工作关系，如果你们想超出这一界限的话，请在工作之外进行。

可能的话，要指出他们的行为已经影响到了办公室里的其他人，这样可以确保他们无法反驳你，或者是说你“多管闲事”、“老保守”、“假正经”。

● ________部门的多位员工已经对你们的行为表示不满了。

● 当________领客户进办公室时，你们还在公然亲热，这让我们所有的人都很难堪。

● 由于你们在整个会议中不断地开玩笑和打情骂俏，导致其他人都抱怨很难集中注意力。

一定要依据其他人亲口说出的自身感受，而不能是你所认为的他们的感受。

- 顾问们说，他们觉得你们两个“很讨厌”。
- 客户说他对有人在办公室里做出这样的行为感到震惊。
- 在会议开始之前，我的团队成员就已经在议论你们之间的关系了。

向老板汇报这一行为

- ________和________在以非职业的方式交往，这在客户面前造成了不良影响。
- 除非________和________能记得按时回来上班，否则的话我们只能让他们分别午休了。
- ________和________在长时间说笑，________办公室已有多人向我们投诉此事了。

避免使用评判性的词语，那样将会削弱你的观点。

- 他们的行为真让人恶心。
- 坦率地说，我认为他们这样做太粗俗了。
- 他们幼稚得可笑。
- 我认为他们使公司蒙羞。

制止他们

- 请原谅，我们正在工作。
- 你们两个不能再这么做了，这让所有的人难堪。
- 如果你们想谈情说爱的话就去别处。
- 请你们尊重一下我们办公室的职业操守。

向碰巧路过的客户或其他人解释这一行为

- 请原谅，我一定会找他们谈话。
- 我们确实是一个很职业的部门，他们这样做一定会受到惩处。
- 很抱歉让您看到这样的事，他们实际上都是很优秀的员工，但是他们之间的关系看起来是出格了。

● 他们这样做很可笑，您走之后我一定通知他们的经理，并且我向您保证他们不会再出现这种行为。

小提示

当讨论恋情或其他非职业交往时，最好用正式用语。实际上，语言越笼统、描述性词汇越少越好。这与通常的商务公文相反。以下是一些正确和错误用语的例子，由此您可以联想出一些其他的说法。

错误用语：

- 约会
- 交往
- 有暧昧关系
- 好色的、性爱的、色欲的

正确用语：

- 行为不正当
- 有非职业关系
- 彼此接触
- 非工作时间在一起

老板不正当地向你表示好感

这种情况的确很麻烦，你并不想接受这些示好行为，而且你根本没有要求这些。问题的严重性在于，老板有权决定你的加薪、晋升，并且在很多方面决定着你的未来。显然你不应该屈服于此，也不应该就此换工作。为什么要离开自己喜爱的工作和同事呢？你应该控制局面，必要时寻求帮助，并继续在事业上获得成功。以下措辞将对你有所帮助。

直接面对老板

事发当场对话用语

● 请您记住我是一名员工，我们之间是工作关系，并且将一直保持这种关系。

● 不，我不能和您一起出去吃晚饭，我想我们之间保持严格的工作关系。

● 我从不和职场中的人约会。

● 我希望把自己的私人生活与工作分开。

随后的电子邮件用语

如果你的老板试图报复或者恶习不改，这封电子邮件可以作为证据保存。

● 在您的办公室里，您……您已经不是第一次这样做了，在上周开会时，您……还有在周五会议结束时，我与同事分手后，您……请尊重我的职业底线。

● 就如我先前在您办公室里所说的，除了工作关系之外，我对其他任何形式的关系都不感兴趣。我不想再提此事，希望您也一样。

● 您在今天早些时候所说的……令我很反感，请尊重我的职业底线。

如果老板送你礼物

● 我把________退还给您，这是您今天早晨放在我抽屉里的。请您注意：作为一名员工，我不能接受这一类的礼物。

● 您放在我桌子上的________很漂亮，但我们必须保持严格的工作关系，从任何角度来说都是如此。

● 您放在我信箱里的________令我很震惊，但是我们之间的关系必须是完全职业性的。由于________很容易变质，为了防止浪费我就不返还给您了，我会把它放在餐厅里供大家分享。

为此事留档

每一次见面或谈话都应该留有记录，这一点很重要，因为你的老板可能会按他的一面之词描述此事并对你不利。要清楚地记录时间、日期以及你们之间的言语和动作。如果有人目击此事或者有同样的经历，也要一并记录下来。

要细致

- ________日早晨，老板叫我去他的办公室，然后他开始……我立刻告诉他，这种行为是不正当的，并且离开了他的办公室。________看到了我离开，并且问我发生了什么事，我没有回答。
- 在________日________时，老板做了如下动作……这已经是第二次了，第一次发生在________时。两次我都告诉他，在工作场合非职业的行为是错误的，尤其是对一名员工更不能如此。
- 老板给我送了花，并且在赠言卡里写道："……。"我随后立即给他发了电子邮件，并重申我们之间只能是工作关系。赠言卡和电子邮件都保留在我的文件夹里。

注意：把材料复印一份放在家里，以防老板搜查你的文件，并且销毁它们。

记录要清晰并且不带个人感情色彩，即使是在描述自身的感受时也要如此。

错误用语：

- 我被他所说的话吓得直发抖。
- 我觉得他真让人恶心。
- 听他说了这种话，真想去洗个澡。
- 我觉得他是我所知道的最令人反感的人。

正确用语：

- 当我说话时，我的声音在发抖。
- 我快速离开了办公室，________问我发生了什么事。

- 我立刻把手从他的手里抽了出来，拿起我的笔记本离开了办公室。
- 我受到了惊吓，并且大叫了起来。

尽量直接引用双方的对话

- 当我走进他的办公室时，他说："……。"
- 他那样做之后，我说："……。"他回答我说："……。"
- 我对他说："……。"在随后的电子邮件中我说了同样的话。

将此事汇报给人事部门

给人事部发一封电子邮件要求一次会面，要确保这一保密的会谈是面对面的。以下完美措辞可用来讨论这一难题。

- 我和老板之间有一些问题，他有一些不正当的冒犯行为……
- 我的老板近来一直在骚扰我，尽管我告诉他说我只想保持工作关系，他的献媚行为仍在继续。比如……
- 我的老板对我……例如，在________日他……我已经告诉他我对此毫无兴趣，并且发了多封电子邮件。这些电子邮件都留存在我的文件夹里。

同事向你献殷勤

如果同事向你献殷勤，你将面临的损害比你想象的还要大。所以，要小心地使用完美措辞来应对。是的，你可以让对方走开，但是要注意：对方可能会去散布谣言、在工作中纠缠你甚至骚扰你，或者是由于你的拒绝而产生敌意。以下是一些应对方法。

要明确地、毫不含糊地表态

初次发生

- 我不相信"职场恋情"，所以请别再找我了。
- 你需要检点自己的行为。

● 不，对不起，但我不想和你交往。我不想把工作关系和私人关系搅在一起，尤其是不能和约会这种事搅在一起。

再次发生

● 不要再用这种方式与我说话，请你尊重我。如果你不这样做的话，我将采取必要的行动。

● 不要以任何理由碰我身体的任何部位，这在工作场合是不正当的。

● 我已经说过了，不会和你约会，在工作之中和工作之外都不会，所以别再提这件事了。

情况仍在持续

● 我在________时和________时告诉过你，请你尊重我的底线，别再打扰我。如果你再冒犯我的话，我就叫保安。

● 我已经明确地告诉过你，我不感兴趣，而你却不停地骚扰我，所以我要举报你。

● 这是我最后一次警告你，你必须停止对我说那样的话，否则我就报警。

小提示

如果你威胁同事说要做某件事的话，一定要确保自己真的是想要这样做，并且付诸实施。如果你的同事威胁你的话，哪怕只有一次，也要立刻举报他。

记录下事件的过程

就像其他由同事或上级给你带来的困境一样，要清楚、详细地将此事记录下来。

● ________日，________问我是否愿意……我告诉他这种话很不合适，他大笑，并且在当天的晚些时候又说了这种话。我的同事________和________碰巧听到了这些话，并且将会支持我的观点。

- ________说，如果我当晚不和他一起开车回家的话，他就对别人说：“……。”
- 上周有三次，分别是在……他说了很粗鲁的话，包括……
- 尽管我告诉________要尊重我的个人空间和职业底线，他上周仍然两次……一次是在________时，另一次是在________时。

在每次遭遇之后，询问其他同事是否听到了相关对话，如果听到了，询问他们是否愿意在老板或人事部门调查此事时为你作证。

向老板汇报此事

- 我和________之间有些问题，请您为我调解一下。
- ________在办公室里骚扰我，我可以举出最近发生的两个事例，并且能证明这些事……
- 最近，________在办公室里以不正当的方式接近我，同样的事在工作之外也发生过，第一次是在……
- ________最近说了……的话，我对他说过如果他不停止的话就向您汇报。

一定要把与老板的谈话记录下来，记住，在这种情况下，你的老板有责任采取行动。

客户以下流的、粗鲁的或其他不正当的行为骚扰你或者你的员工

这种讨厌的客户远不止是讨厌而已，他是在骚扰你和你的员工。但是，正是该人在向你们付费，并且提供了新的利润来源。那么该怎么办呢？是让对方见鬼去还是对这种行为委曲求全？都不是。从以下完美措辞中可以找到答案。要以最明确、最职业的方式采取行动，并且寄希望于对方能尊重这种姿态。

避开对方礼貌的示好

- 谢谢，但我并不这么认为。
- 不，谢谢。我们公司有规定，在工作场合此类事情是禁止的，即使谈论一下都不行。
- 感谢您的邀请，但我不能接受。
- 我知道这一定很有趣，但我最好还是不这样做。
- 不，对不起，我不和在工作中认识的人约会。

如果是以书面的形式回复，要抄送给老板和 / 或人事部门，以防客户报复或者是曲解你的回复，甚至企图让你被解雇。

应对下流的或者冒失的言语

- 这是在工作场合，我们必须保持一种职业的氛围。
- 我不欣赏此类的话。
- 在工作场合，此类话是无法让人接受的，请别再说了。
- 请不要在我或者我的客户面前使用这样的语言。
- 别对我说那样的话。
- 我对这种话不感兴趣，请不要再说了。

坚决让客户停止不当行为

- 您必须马上停止说这种事，否则的话我们将禁止您入内。
- 这里是职业场合，您必须遵守我们的规定，否则的话我们将拒绝为您服务。
- 如果您还想说这种话，就请您不要再来了。
- 当您说这种话时，我的客户很难堪，并且我的员工也感觉受到了侮辱，你必须马上停止。

要求客户离开

如果是在室内，要低声、清楚地要求其离开，要使该客户能听清楚的同时防止其他人注意到此事。如果你是在为一家大机构服务，并且有保安人员的话，要提醒其注意并表示你不想惊动其他客户。如果不是这样，可与当地公安机关联系，告诉他们你可能会遇到麻烦，必要时请求其派人来提供帮助。

- 对不起，但您必须离开这里。如果您不走的话，我就叫保安。
- 请您体面、安静地离开这里，我不想叫保安，这对您和其他人来说都不好。
- 您必须离开我们的办公室，这儿所有的人都为您的语气感到不安。
- 您必须马上离开，我已经报了警，他们正在赶来。所以，请马上离开，以免使您和其他人难堪。

发电子邮件通知客户不要再来了

- 对不起，但我们必须警告您：由于您的……行为，您将被禁止进入我公司。
- 请注意：我们已经通知保安人员，禁止您再次进入我们的办公场所。
- 如……所示，由于在________和________所发生的事故，您被禁止进入我们的办公场所。如果您需要办理业务的话，请给________发电子邮件，邮箱是________。

确保你没有冒犯或者侮辱该客户，要尽量采用职业的语气。

错误用语：

- 你是个卑劣的人。
- 这儿的所有人都不想再见到你，所以请别再来了。
- 我们确实痛恨你所带来的一切麻烦。
- 你真让人恶心。
- 你是个可怜虫。
- 你病得不轻，应该去看精神病医生。

正确用语：

- 你的行为干扰了我的员工。

- 你出言不逊，尽管我们要求你别再这样做，你却依然如故。
- 你大声说了这些不适当的言语，激怒了我们的客户和员工。
- 这种冒犯已经在会议上引起了争执，所以我们的顾问无法继续进行此项目。

应对下流的电子邮件

不要回复，直接将该发件人列入黑名单。但是，要发邮件给保安人员，让他们知道你要禁止该客户在办公场地出现。邮件可以这样写：

- 我从一个客户那收到了一封这样的邮件，我要禁止他进入我方办公场地。
- 我们中的几个人都收到了来自客户的色情邮件，我们打算屏蔽掉他的邮件，同时要禁止他进入我们的办公场所，我们该怎么做？
- 我们的一个客户发送了这样的邮件，员工感觉到了不安，害怕他会来到公司使我们难堪。我们该怎么做？
- 对于发送此邮件的客户，我们要禁止其进入大楼。

当客户方的员工粗鲁、下流或者捣乱

发邮件约时间讨论此事

- 我们与您的一位员工之间有些问题，希望得到您的帮助。
- 您能否代表我们和您的一位员工谈一次话。
- 我们有必要和您谈一谈关于你方的一名员工的问题。

小提示

当直接挑明主题时，自己要明确想从客户那里得到什么样的结果，是通过谈话使该员工停止不当行为，还是希望换掉他。

希望制止不当行为

- 您的员工________有……行为记录，例如，在……他……您能否就此与他谈谈？制止他的这种行为。
- 您能否让您的员工________停止……我们的多位同事对此行为不满，并且感觉与他一起工作很不舒服。

希望换掉该人

- 您的一位员工________，曾对我方员工……所以，我们将禁止他再次进入我们的办公室。
- 尽管我们曾经制止，但您的员工________在几次会议中一直……所以，我们必须禁止他再次进入我们的办公室。
- ________曾在我们的办公室里……显而易见，这种行为使我方员工很不舒服。尽管我欣赏________的工作，但我必须保护自己的员工，并且要求您调换人员。
- 您能否另派一名员工来我们办公室工作以接替________？他曾经……影响了我方员工。

员工在工作时间使用不适当的材料或登陆成人网站

很难想象，超过半数的网上色情信息都是在办公场所被浏览的。当然，工作之外的所作所为是员工自己的事，但是在办公室里，这就要引发特殊的问题。显然，员工应该专心工作而不是浏览成人网站，而且其他员工或者客户可能会看到这些信息并产生反感，还可能更糟。所以，对此一定不能掉以轻心，要马上处理。

直接面对当事人

告诉该员工你是怎么知道他在看这种东西的，这样对方就不能抵赖了。然后告诉当事人不能再这样做，必要的话，告诉对方你下一步打算如何处理。

- 我在你的电脑屏幕上看到了一些色情图片，这令我和其他人很反感。别再看这种东西了。
- 多名员工投诉说曾在你的电脑屏幕上看到过色情图片。在工作场合，你不能以任何方式看这种东西。
- 在维修你的电脑时，我们的技术人员发现你登录过色情网站。你知道，在工作场合这样做是不当的。你不能再做此类事，否则我将采取处罚措施。

向经理汇报

● 本周，我多次在________的电脑屏幕上看到了色情图片，您能否就此与他谈一下？

● ________在工作时看色情视频，我是由……知道此事的。以我的身份不适合处理此事，希望您能对此采取措施。

● 我和几位同事都在________的电脑屏幕上看到过色情图片，作为我们的经理，我认为应该让您了解此事。

● 我觉得应该向您汇报一下，________在工作时间看色情图片，这使我很反感，但我的身份不适合处理此事。

当你身为一家大公司的经理，并且该公司有明确的行为准则

你必须保护那些向你投诉的员工，同时也要让被投诉的员工明白别人已经注意到其不良行为了。

● 有多位员工向我反映，你在工作时间看色情内容。我们明文规定禁止这种行为，屡次犯错将被开除。这是对你的第一次警告。

● 我注意到你在办公时间看色情材料。根据________政策，有此类行为的员工可以不经警告即行开除。考虑到你在其他方面是一名优秀的员工，我再给你一次机会。

● 我们公司的政策（员工手册中的行为准则部分）规定，禁止员工在工作场所观看色情或其他成人材料。有多名员工向我反映你看了此类材料，并且用电子邮件在办公室里传播色情图片。如果再发生此事，我们就不得不解雇你。

小提示

最好是用电子邮件传达此类信息，这样，你就会留有一份记录。如果是面谈此事，也要随后发一封电子邮件，确认你的谈话内容。

作为一家小公司的管理人员，并且公司没有明确的行为准则

- 我刚刚获知你在工作时间看色情材料，这会影响其他员工并且会造成不良的工作氛围。你必须马上停止这样做，否则我将开除你。
- 我刚刚获知你在看色情电影，并且在你的桌子上发现了色情材料。由于有员工在此前发现过你有此类行为，并且这种行为干扰正常的工作环境。所以，你必须离职，等待我的下一步处理。
- 有多位员工举报，你在工作时间使用色情材料。如果我再接到此类投诉或者见到此类行为，我就解雇你。请注意，你的电脑是公司财产，我有权检查。我将检查你的电脑，确保你不再出现此类行为。

Part Eight

Relationship Quagmires

No kidding. You shouldn't have love affairs at work. You shouldn't watch sexy movies on the Web. And you shouldn't e-mail your beloved during company time. But face it, we're human, right? Actually, no. At work, we have to set certain aspects of our humanness aside, at least temporarily, so we can thrive as professionals. In fact, romance acts as putty sticking to our feet, keeping us in place, and, depending on the romance, creating a big mess.

But what happens when cupid slings his arrows in the workplace. What do you say to the coworkers who are smitten? And what about those altogether unwanted gestures from the guy who flirts at the copy machine or the unwanted candy and flowers your boss sent you? Ignoring these situations is foolish, unlikely, or even impossible. So here are a few pointers followed by perfect phrases you can't do without:

- **Measure the offense.** Romantic situations at work have various degrees of seriousness, and you should act according to the circumstances involved in each of them. If a person asks you out on a date and you say no, that's one thing. If he or she keeps pestering, that's more serious. If that person follows you home, sends you e-mails, or makes kissing sounds as you pass, that's harassment.

  Of course, employees who reveal their affections at the proverbial water cooler can be equally and unhealthily distracting. So determine the degree of the offense, and react in kind.

- **Report to the right source.** In some cases—possibly many cases—you may need to report the difficult situation to an authority. Only, pick your authority carefully. If you're a woman and your boss is a man, he may not be responsive to your complaints that a male is pestering you. Similarly, if you tell a manager of either gender, he or she may not be aware of the steps you should take. Instead, you may need to consult with your HR Department or even an attorney before taking steps.

● **Be clear about the outcome you want.** What is the outcome you want? For the behavior to end? For the offensive couple to move to a different part of the building—or the planet? Or do think the employee deserves more serious forms of punishment, including a lawsuit? You may need clarity about what you're thinking or feeling to get a better perspective about what you want. So before you communicate with anyone, get a strong sense of your own intentions.

When Two Employees Are Having an Affair

Okay, so the employees are having a love affair. Or maybe it's a sordid affair. Who knows? And frankly, it's none of your business—or anyone else's. Except that they make it so obvious. You know the syrupy glances, the muffled conversations, and the inappropriate gestures in the parking lot. If this were high school, all right. But it isn't, and their interactions are distracting to everyone on your team. So they better cool it, and these perfect phrases will certainly help.

When Addressing One of the Amorous Employees

● If you and _____ are interested in each other in a nonprofessional way, please be more discreet.

● If you want to make so much noise chatting and laughing, you should wait until work ends. It's distracting to people.

● You and ____ need to keep your workplace relationship as professional as possible. If you want to go beyond those limitations, do so after hours.

When possible, mention the effect their behavior is having on other people in the office. This will ensure that they won't dismiss your complaint by calling you a "busybody," "uptight," or a "prude."

● Several people from the ____ department have complained about your behavior.

● Apparently you were carrying on when ____ brought a client into the office. We were all embarrassed.

● Because both of you were making jokes and insinuations throughout the meeting, people complained that they had a hard time focusing.

Be sure to rely on what other people said they felt—not on what you believe they felt:

● The consultants said they find the two of you "annoying."

● Our customer said he was "surprised" that people in our office carry on that way.

● People on my team were commenting on your relationship before the meeting started.

When Discussing That Behavior with Your Boss

● ___ and ____ have been touching each other in a nonprofessional manner. This poses problems in front of customers.

● We need to make sure that ___ and ____ either take separate lunch breaks or remember to return to the office on time.

● ___ and ___ have been having long conversations that involved lots of laughing. Several people from the ___ office complained to us about it.

Steer clear of judgmental language that might weaken your point:

● They're behavior is disgusting.

● Frankly, I think it's gross that they behave this way.

● They're being ridiculously immature.

● I think they're an embarrassment to the company.

When Interrupting Them in the Act

● Excuse me, but we are at work.

● You two have to cut this out. It's embarrassing to everyone.

● Go somewhere else if you feel amorous.

● Would you mind respecting the professionalism of our office?

When Explaining That Behavior to a Client or Someone Else Who Happens to Be Passing By

● Excuse them. I need to have a talk with them.

- We're actually a professional organization—they won't get away with behavior like that.
- Sorry you had to see that. They're both actually great employees, but their relationship seems to have gotten out of hand.
- They're being goofy. After you leave, I'll let their manager know, and I can assure you they'll stop.

Quick tip

When discussing romantic or otherwise nonprofessional interactions, better stick to formal language. In fact, the less description and the more general, the better. This is the antithesis of what you generally try to achieve in business writing. Here's a list of dos and don'ts phrases. Let your imagination do the rest.

Don't

- Dating each other
- Going out
- Having an affair
- Being erotic, sexual, or sensual

Do

- Acting inappropriately
- Having a nonprofessional relationship
- Touching each other
- Being together in a social context

When You Receive Inappropriate Overtures from a Boss

This situation is obviously problematic. You don't want the overtures and didn't ask for them in the first place. Even more, your boss has power over your raises, promotion potential, and, in many ways, your future. Obviously, you shouldn't yield. Nor should you decide you'll find another job. Why leave behind colleagues and work that you love? Instead, you should take control, get support if you need it, and continue moving ahead. These phrases will help support you.

When Confronting the Boss

At the Moment of the Advance

● Remember I'm an employee, and our relationship is and will remain professional.

● No, I won't be able to go out for dinner—I prefer to keep our relationship strictly professional.

● I never date anyone at work.

● I like to keep my private life separate.

In an E-Mail Later

This e-mail should also serve as documentation if your boss attempts to retaliate or doesn't change the behavior.

● In your office, you z. This is not the first time you have done this; in our meeting last week you ______, and on Friday, as I was leaving after the meeting with my team, you _____. Please respect my professional boundaries.

● As I stated in your office earlier today, I am not interested in any type of nonprofessional relationship at work. I will not bring this subject up again and assume the same holds true for you.

● I found the comment that you made earlier today "______" troubling. Please respect my professional boundaries.

If He or She Sends You a Gift

● I am returning the _____ that you left in my desk drawer this morning. Please recognize that as an employee, I cannot accept this type of gift.

● Although the _____ that you left at my desk were beautiful, we need to maintain a strictly professional relationship in every sense.

● The _____ that you left in my mailbox was quite a surprise, but my relationship with you must be clearly professional. Since _____ is perishable, and will only spoil if I give it back, I will leave it in the lunch room for everyone to share.

When Documenting the Event

It's critical that you document every interaction since the situation could come down to your boss's word against yours. Be clear about times, dates, and the gestures or words that passed between you. If anyone witnessed the event or has had similar experiences, be sure to document that, too.

Be Specific

- The morning of ____, the boss called me into his room. Then he proceeded to _____. I immediately told him his behavior was inappropriate and left the room. ____ saw me leaving and asked what was wrong. I didn't respond.
- On ___ at ____, the boss did the following: _____, _____, and _____. This was the second time this occurred. The first time was on ____. Both times I said that unprofessional behavior was wrong in the workplace, especially toward an employee.
- The boss sent me flowers with the words_____ on the card. I e-mailed him immediately after to restate that my relationship is professional. The card and e-mail are in my files.

Note: Be sure to leave a copy of your documentation at home, just in case the boss should rummage through your files to delete them.

Be clear and emotion-free—even when discussing your feelings.

Don't

- I was horrified and sickened by what he said.
- I think she is disgusting.
- After he said that, I wanted to take a shower.
- I think she is the most revolting person I know.

Do

- When I spoke, my voice was shaking.
- I left the room so quickly, ___ asked me what was wrong.
- I removed my hand from his immediately, took my notebook, and left the room.

- I was so surprised, I shouted.

Use Direct Quotes Where Possible

- When I entered his office, he said: "________________."
- After he did that, I said: "______." He said: "_______________" back to me.
- I told him then, and in my follow-up e-mail: "______________________."

When Bringing the Issue to Your HR Department

E-mail HR that you want to establish a meeting, but make sure the confidential conversation is face-to-face. Here are some perfect phrases for discussing this difficult situation:

- I am having some problems with my boss. He has been making inappropriate advances . . .
- My boss has been harassing me recently. Although I tell her that I only want a professional relationship, the advances continue. For example, on . . .
- My boss has been _____, _____, and _____. For example, on _____ he . . . I have told him that I had no interest and sent several e-mails. These are in my file.

When a Coworker Comes On to You

When a coworker makes advances, you have more to lose than you think, so use the perfect phrases with care. Yes, you can tell your coworker to buzz off, but beware. He or she might spread rumors, pester or even harass you during the workday, or get hostile because you rebuffed him or her. Here are some ideas of what to do.

Be Clear and Unambiguous

The First Time a Situation Occurs

- I do not believe in workplace relationships, so please don't ask me again.
- You need to keep your hands to yourself.
- No, I'm sorry, but I am not interested in going out with you. I do not mix professional and personal relationships, especially with dates.

The Next Time a Situation Occurs

● Don't ever talk to me that way again. I demand respect, and if you don't give it, I will take action.

● Do not touch me anywhere or for any reason. This is inappropriate at work.

● As I said, I will not go out with you—during or after work—so please don't bring it up.

If the Situation Persists

● I told you on _____ and ____ that you should respect my boundaries and leave me alone. If you invade my space one more time, I will contact security.

● I am going to report you because you keep pursuing me although I have been clear that I am not interested.

● This is my last warning. You must stop making comments like that to me, or I will report you to security.

Quick tip

If you threaten a coworker, make sure you mean it. And yes, do follow up. If your coworker threatens you, even once, report this person immediately.

Document the Interactions

Like any situation where an employee or manager is giving you a hard time, be sure to document in clear and specific terms:

● On _____, _____ asked me if I would _____. When I said that kind of language was inappropriate, he laughed and repeated the comment later that day. My coworkers, ____ and _____, overheard the comment and will support me in this claim.

● _____ said that if I didn't drive home with her that night, she would tell people that "____________."

● Three times last week, on ____, ____, and ____, he made rude comments including ______.

● Although I told _____ to respect my space and my professional boundaries, she ________ twice last week, once on ____ and the other time on _____.

After an encounter, ask fellow coworkers if they overheard the interaction. If so, ask if they'd be witnesses if your boss, or someone in HR, asks.

Discuss the Situation with Your Boss

- I have been having trouble with _____, and you need to intervene for me.
- _____ has been harassing me in the office. I have two examples that occurred recently and can illustrate the problem______.
- Recently, ____ has been approaching me on matters that are inappropriate for the office and, for that matter, outside of work. The first time this occurred . . .
- _____ recently said ____ and ____. I told him that I would talk to you unless he stopped.

Be sure to document the conversation with your boss. And remember, your boss is responsible for taking action in a case like this.

When a Client Bothers You or Your Employees through Lewd, Rude, or Other Inappropriate Behavior

That bothersome client is more than bothersome. He or she is harassing you or your employee. Yet that person also pays the bills and brings in a renewed source of profit. So what now? Do you tell the client to get lost? Or do you tiptoe your way around the poor behavior? The answer, as you'll see from these perfect phrases, is neither. You act in the clearest and most professional manner and hope that he or she respects that position.

When Warding Off Polite Overtures

- Thanks, but I don't think so.
- No, thank you—we have company policies that prohibit us from even discussing the issue at work.
- I appreciate the offer, but no.
- I'm sure it would be fun, but I better not.
- No, I'm sorry. I don't date people I know through work.

If you respond in writing to any overtures, blind "cc" your boss and/or someone in human resources. You never know—the client may get irritated and misrepresent your response or, worse, try to get you fired.

When Addressing Lewd or Forward Comments

● This is a workplace, and we must maintain a professional atmosphere.

● I don't appreciate those kinds of comments.

● Comments like that are unacceptable at work. Please don't repeat them again.

● Please do not use language like that in front of me or my customers.

● Do not speak to me like that.

● I have no interest in hearing those kinds of comments. Please stop immediately.

When Insisting That a Client Stop Repeated Inappropriate Behavior

● You must stop saying things like that immediately, or we won't be able to let you in.

● This is a professional environment, and you must abide by our policies or we'll have to refuse you service.

● Do not come in again if you plan to say things like that again.

● When you say things like that, you are embarrassing our customers and humiliating our employees. You must stop at once.

When Telling the Client to Leave

When in the building, speak quietly yet clearly, so the client can hear you but no one else detects the problem. If you work for a large organization and have a security guard, tell that person to be alert. If not, contact the local police department, say that you might be having trouble, and ask if someone could come by to assist, if necessary. Remind security personnel that you don't want to upset your customers.

● I'm sorry, but you'll have to leave the building. If you don't, we'll call security.

● Please leave the building quietly and respectfully. I don't want to embarrass you or anyone else by having to call security.

● You need to leave our office. Your tone of voice is disruptive to everyone here.

● You must go right now. I have alerted the police, and they're on the way. So avoid embarrassing yourself or anyone else and leave now.

When Telling a Client by E-Mail Not to Return

● I'm sorry, but we must warn you that you are no longer allowed on our premises because of your behavior on ___, ____, and ____.

● Please note that we have alerted our security officer that you are no longer permitted in our building.

● As of ___, you are no longer allowed in our building because of the incidents on ___ and ___. If you need to finish any business, please e-mail ____, at______.

Make sure that you do not insult or humiliate the client; keep the most professional tone possible.

Don't

● You are a despicable person.

● Everyone here hates the sight of you, so just don't come in again.

● We really resent all the disruptions you've caused.

● You're sick.

● You're pathetic.

● You have serious problems and need to see a shrink.

Do

● Your behavior has been upsetting our employees.

● Your comments are insulting. Although we told you to stop, you have persisted nonetheless.

● You have said these inappropriate comments loudly, upsetting our customers and our employees.

● These insults have created disruptions during the meeting. As a result, our consultants have been unable to move forward with the project.

When Responding to Indecent E-Mails

Don't respond—just make sure that person's e-mails head straight to your spam filter. But do alert security and let them know you don't want the customer on the premises again by forwarding an e-mail that says this:

- I have been receiving e-mails like this one from a customer. I don't want him on the premises again.
- Several of us have been receiving explicit e-mails from our customer. We're going to block her e-mails from getting through, but also need to ensure that she is not allowed in the building. What should we do?
- One of our customers has been sending e-mails like this one. The employees feel threatened and are concerned that he will come on the premises and embarrass us. What should we do?
- We need to stop the customer who sent this from entering our building.

When a Client's Employee Is Rude, Lewd, or Disruptive

When Arranging a Time to Talk through an E-Mail

- We have been having a problem with one of your employees and were hoping you can help.
- Could you please talk to one of your employees on our behalf?
- We need to talk to you about one of your employees.

Quick tip

When addressing the topic directly, make sure you know exactly what you want the client to do as a result. Talk to the employee so the behavior stops? Replace that employee with another one?

When You Want the Bad Behavior to Stop

- Your employee ____ has a history of ____. For example, on ____ he _____. Could you please discuss this behavior with him so it stops?
- Could you please tell your employee _____ to stop _____. Several of my coworkers have complained about this behavior and feel uncomfortable working with her as a result.

When You Want the Employee to Stop Coming to Your Office

- One of your employees, ______, has been _______ our employees. So we cannot let him into our office again.

● In several of our meetings, your employee ___, has insisted on ____, although we have asked her to stop. As a result, we must request that she doesn't return to our office.

● ____ has been ______ in our office. Understandably, this makes my employees uncomfortable. While I like ___'s work, I must protect my employees and request that you bring in a replacement.

● Could you please send another employee to our office instead of ___. He has been _____, making my employees uncomfortable.

When an Employee Uses Inappropriate Materials or Accesses Adult Web Sites at Work

Hard to imagine, but more than half of online pornography is viewed in the workplace. What a person does outside of work is his or her business, of course, but inside the office, this poses unique problems. Obviously, the employee should be engaged in work, not adult viewing. As well, other employees or clients may catch sight of the material and feel uncomfortable or worse. So better not shrug and ignore the problem—but address it immediately.

When Confronting the Employee Directly

State how you know the employee views the material, so he or she can't say you're making false accusations. Then tell that person to stop. If necessary, tell him or her what you'll do next.

● I noticed some explicit images on your computer screen. This makes me and other people uncomfortable, and you should stop.

● Several employees have complained that they've seen explicit images on your computer screen. You must stop viewing this material in any form while at work.

● While repairing your computer, our technical assistant found that you have bookmarked explicit Web sites. As you know, this is inappropriate for the workplace. You must stop doing this, or I will have to take disciplinary measures.

When Notifying a Manager

● Several times this week, I've noticed explicit images on ____'s computer screen. Could you confront him or her on this matter?

● ____ watches explicit videos at work. I know this because______. I do not feel it is my place to say anything and was hoping you'd take action.

● As my manager, I thought you should know that several of my coworkers and I have seen explicit images on ____'s computer screen.

● I thought you should know that ____views explicit images at work. While this makes me uncomfortable, I do not feel it's my position to say anything.

When You Are the Manager in a Large Company with Policies Dictating Behavior

While you must protect the employees who told you about the situation, be sure the person knows that others are aware of the situation, as well.

● Several employees have informed me that you have been viewing explicit material during work hours. Our policy states that this is unacceptable and grounds for dismissal. So take this as your first warning.

● I noticed that you are viewing explicit material on company time. According to policy ______, employees who engage in this behavior can be fired without a warning. Since you are an otherwise good employee, though, I am willing to give you another chance.

● Our company policy, under the Codes of Behavior section of our handbook, states that employees are not allowed to view explicit or other adult materials in the workplace. Several employees have notified me that you have been viewing these sorts of materials and e-mailing images around the office. If this occurs one more time, we will be forced to fire you.

Remember

It's always best to e-mail this kind of message so you have a record. If you discuss it face-to-face, send an e-mail afterward, confirming your discussion.

When You Are the Manager in a Small Company without Policies Dictating Behavior

● I have just learned that you are viewing explicit material at work. This intimidates other employees and creates an uncomfortable work environment. You must stop at once, or I will be forced to fire you.

● I just learned that you have been viewing explicit behavior and have explicit materials at your desk. Because one of our employees spoke to you about this previously, and because this creates a difficult environment for us all, you must leave the office until I determine the next steps.

● Several employees have commented on your use of explicit materials at work. If I hear another complaint or see any indication, I will fire you. Be aware that your computer is company property and I can, and will, access it to make sure you have not repeated this behavior.